ESSENTIAL
FENG
SHUI

林碧盆
朱
LILLIAN
TOO

For Rinpoche

For Jennifer
For Wan Jin
For all sentient beings.

LILLIAN TOO'S ESSENTIAL FENG SHUI

A STEP-BY STEP GUIDE TO ENHANCING YOUR RELATIONSHIPS, HEALTH AND PROSPERITY

RIDER

LONDON · SYDNEY · AUCKLAND · JOHANNESBURG

First published in 1998

1 3 5 7 10 8 6 4 2

Published in 1998 by Rider,
an imprint of Ebury Press, Random House,
20 Vauxhall Bridge Road, London SW1V 2SA

Random House Australia (Pty) Limited
20 Alfred Street, Milsons Point Sydney,
New South Wales 2061, Australia

Random House New Zealand Limited
18 Poland Road, Glenfield,
Auckland 10, New Zealand

Random House South Africa (Pty) Limited
Endulni, 5A Jubilee Road, Parktown 2193, South Africa

Random House UK Limited Reg. No. 954009

Papers used by Rider Books are natural, recyclable products made from
wood grown from sustainable forests.

Printed by

A CIP catalogue record for this book is available from the British
Library

ISBN 0-7126-7162-5

Contents

Foreword

Feng shui is an ancient Chinese science, which prescribes ways of living in a state of harmony and balance with your personal environment in order to enjoy great good fortune. It is a technique of arranging your living space, a method of managing your surroundings, of arranging layouts and furniture. Feng shui prescribes auspicious orientations for harnessing mysterious metaphysical forces that float in the air and the space that surround us. Practitioners describe these forces as chi and colourfully describe it as the dragon's cosmic breath.

Chinese who practice feng shui strive to surround themselves with auspicious chi. They believe that when their home is located, orientated and arranged to create a maximum amount of chi, that this celestial breath will assure them of good fortune. A home that enjoys good chi benefits every member of the family, particularly the head of the household. When the location of the home is auspiciously surrounded by the four celestial animals – the dragon, the tiger, the tortoise and the phoenix – then good fortune is perpetuated from descendant to descendant for at least five generations.

Feng shui in China

For centuries, feng shui was practised by the ruling classes of Imperial China. At least from the time of the Tang dynasty to the last Ching emperors, feng shui remained an important part of Imperial court practice and feng shui masters were either revered for their highly respected knowledge or put to death to ensure others would not use their knowledge against the son of heaven. In an atmosphere of continuous court intrigues, emperors guarded their feng shui experts with cunning and care. Chinese folk tales are filled with stories of feng shui divinations that accompanied the formation of new dynasties. For instance, the first Ming emperor, Chu Yuan Chuan – a ruffian, a beggar and a bandit – was believed to have succeeded in overthrowing the last Mongol emperor to create the Ming dynasty precisely because of the extremely auspicious feng shui of his father's grave. However, upon becoming emperor, Chu Yuan Chuan subsequently ordered that all feng shui masters to be put to death, and that fake feng shui books were to be written and distributed through the length and breath of the country.

When Yong Le, the third Ming emperor, started building the new northern capital, what is now the Forbidden City in Beijing, it is believed that his architects and builders used these same fake books to arrange the feng shui of the new palaces. Thus it was that shortly after the new palaces were completed, they burnt to the ground.

The architectural history of the Forbidden City is rich with folk stories of incorrect feng shui causing problems and mishaps. When the Manchus overthrew the Mings and took over in the sixteenth century, they too succumbed to incorrect feng shui until the emperor Chien Lung took a personal interest and succeeded in introducing correct feng shui features. Because it is believed that he enjoyed excellent feng shui, Chien Lung's reign was one of prosperity and good fortune for his people.

In more recent times, it has been speculated that the latter day communist emperors of China – Mao Tse Tung and Deng Xioa Ping – both benefited from the excellent feng shui of their ancestors' graves. Mao's grandfather's grave was said to have resided in the palm of the heavenly moon goddess, a configuration so auspicious it would bring great good fortune to the grandson of the family: in this case, the great helmsman Mao. In Deng's case, the feng shui fable has to do with his father's grave, as well as the presence of three auspicious peaks within sight of the family home.

Unlikely as it seems, feng shui did not flourish in the China of Mao

The dissemination of feng shui

Feng shui crossed the waters to other territories with the Chinese who fled the motherland. Many feng shui masters followed the Kuomintang general Chiang Kai Shek to Taiwan – bringing with them precious texts and invaluable feng shui luo pans, or compasses, which contained the trade secrets of the Masters. Therefore in the early part of this century, the ruling elite and entrepreneurs of Taiwan benefited hugely from excellent feng shui knowledge. It is not a coincidence that Taiwan and the Kuomintang flourished during those years, and even today, Taiwan continues to be one of the richest countries in the world.

Feng shui also crossed into Hong Kong, where intrepid refugees and immigrants fled to build new lives. They, too, brought with them the feng shui knowledge of their forefathers, and like their counterparts in Taiwan, used this ancient body of knowledge to tap into the luck of their new environment.

Today, Taiwan and Hong Kong are acknowledged economic success stories. There are many who attribute their huge success to the almost universal application of feng shui guidelines. Feng shui techniques of spatial arrangement were applied not only in their places of residence but also to offices, workplaces, factories and commercial developments.

Tse Tung. Indeed, during his reign, the practice of feng shui was strictly forbidden. Mao lived his entire life obsessed by the fear of being overthrown, and he was not to risk anyone using feng shui luck to overshadow his own luck!

The changing face of feng shui

In Hong Kong, feng shui masters initially diagnosed only the surrounding environments to ensure auspicious orientations. Building exteriors were orientated to capture the protection of hills and feed from the symbolic wealth of the waters of the harbour. Roads were built in accordance to dragon/tiger symbolism and classical tenets were closely observed. But as the cities grew, as modern buildings mushroomed and urban living took over, feng shui guidelines penetrated into the interiors of buildings and homes, and whole new interpretations of the old tenets began to appear. These adapted to modern living conditions.

Old masters studied their inherited luo pans to find new interpretations to ancient symbols; others deliberated on secret compass formulas and began incorporating them into their practice. At the same time, they experimented with methods against the emerging new environment of city living. Many kept these formulas secret, guarding them jealously and zealously. Old masters passed them on by oral transmissions to favourite disciples or blood relatives.

Master Yap Cheng Hai

I came upon three of these valuable formulas at various stages of my life, and have used them for my own benefit for many years. They were given to me by my dear friend Master Yap Cheng Hai, an acknowledged feng shui expert who has spent the better part of thirty years making many people extremely wealthy and happy in Malaysia. Master Yap Cheng Hai is an authentic feng shui master who, as a young man, studied under countless old masters from Hong Kong and Taiwan. Possessed of a native curiosity into all things metaphysical, an awesome intellect, and a photographic memory, Yap Cheng Hai actively sought out masters to learn the secrets of the practice of feng shui.

In his thirty year career as a feng shui master, he has subsequently made many businessmen into truly prosperous billionaires and multi-millionaires. Many continue to be his clients, consulting him on every new corporate project or property development they undertake and benefiting in other ways from Mr Yap's wonderful feng shui advice.

Mr Yap has often intimated to me that enhancing people's incomes is one of the easiest of human aspirations to satisfy with feng shui. But he has also explained that the magnitude of wealth, which results from feng shui, differs from person to person. This depends on what he terms their heaven luck (see page 13). If they do not have the heaven luck to become tycoons or multi-millionaires, for instance, having auspicious wealth feng shui will bring them a life of relative ease where money will not be a problem. But it will not make them into billionaires.

I have also benefited from Mr Yap's income enhancing feng shui methods. I do not have the karma to be a multi-millionaire business tycoon, but indeed, I am more than satisfied with the results. Over the years I have enjoyed good income and have nothing to complain about. In my case, unlike most of Mr Yap's clients, however, I have implemented Mr Yap's feng shui techniques myself. In the beginning, this was because Mr Yap was simply so difficult to get hold of, but increasingly it was because I developed a huge and obsessive curiosity about the subject.

I have called upon my great friendship with Mr Yap and asked him to let me release his feng shui expertise and formulas to the world. My research into the subject has given me a huge respect for the science and I told Mr Yap I would present it as a body of knowledge totally devoid of spiritual or religious connotations. For that has been my finding.

That I succeeded in persuading Yap Cheng Hai is a measure of his great generosity. My whole series of feng shui books has been the result of that generosity for it was he who provided the key to unlocking many of the secrets of the Pa Kua and the Lo Shu numbers, described later in this book, thereby allowing previously unintelligible explanations contained in the old texts and passed on to me by other feng shui practitioners, to become meaningful.

Today, Yap Cheng Hai is well into his seventies. His decision to share his feng shui expertise coincides with a worldwide explosion of interest in this ancient Chinese science. Surely that cannot be a coincidence?

Using feng shui

As a happy beneficiary of Mr Yap's feng shui expertise, and later through my own study and research, I have discovered that feng shui is best approached as a technique. There is nothing magical about the way feng shui works. When the formulas were applied correctly they brought wonderful good fortune into my life. And each time my fortunes took a dip, I always found the reasons in the flying stars that make up yet another feng shui formula.

During my years in Hong Kong I met a great many other feng shui masters and practitioners and I discovered there are many different schools of feng shui, and that there is considerable depth to this seemingly frivolous subject. I decided then to take advantage of my corporate access to experts in China, Hong Kong and Taiwan and make the study of feng shui a serious hobby. At that time I looked on knowledge of feng shui as an additional management tool. It was never my intention to become either a feng shui writer or a feng shui consultant.

It was in later years, after I had retired from the corporate world, and had made the decision to share the wealth of my feng shui knowledge, so generously given to me by so many different masters, that I became a writer. I still do not undertake feng shui consulting, preferring instead to disseminate and teach the knowledge and leaving the consulting to the many excellent exponents of the craft currently engaged in it professionally for a livelihood.

A few years ago, feng shui was almost unknown in the West. Today it enjoys growing mainstream curiosity and appeal. This interest will continue to soar, simply because as more and more people learn to live harmoniously with the environment, and start to materially benefit from it as well, feng shui's popularity will rise. The same potency, which ensured its survival in China through the last four thousand years, will now fuel interest in its practice throughout the modern world.

Learn to use feng shui. Let this old Chinese wisdom teach you the secrets of the living earth. Suspend whatever scepticism you may have for an instant and discover another way of looking at the energies that permeate the environment. Discover depths of meanings in the simplicity of the yin yang cosmology. Tune into the subtleties of the five elements in your surroundings as they interact continuously with each other. Experience the mysterious potency of the living earth's invisible intangible forces as you tap into their energies to bring good luck into your life.

In the process enjoy a better, healthier, happier and richer life.

Lillian Too

Introduction

Feng shui is an ancient Chinese method of living in tune with the energies of the living earth. It is a set of techniques and a body of knowledge that can be studied and then systematically applied to your personal space and environment. When applied correctly, feng shui holds out the promise of creating great good fortune to those who arrange their homes and offices according to its principles of harmony and balance.

Feng shui can seriously enhance your fortunes, improve your material well-being and look after your good health. It directly addresses all the aspirations of mankind, bringing opportunities for advancement and prosperity even as it magnifies chances of achievement, promotion and success.

Feng shui as science and art

But feng shui is not magic. Neither is it a spiritual practice requiring a strong faith in its potency, or a belief in its effectiveness. Feng shui is best approached as a science and practised as an art. It is a science because much of feng shui applications are based on the accurate usage of what are collectively grouped under Compass School feng shui, also broadly known as formula feng shui. Under this system of techniques, building and laying out rooms and furniture in accordance with the orientations of the compass combined with calculations based on formulas bring the desired good fortune. But accuracy of measurement, both of the compass direction (sometimes to the nearest degree), and the correct measurements of dimensions are crucial factors in the success of the practice. If the proportions are accurately measured and the computations have been correctly worked out, formula feng shui almost always works by improving the luck of residents. Results do not take long to manifest. But also remember that if practised incorrectly, feng shui simply does not work!

Much of feng shui is also an art that requires subjective judgement and interpretation. Experience is a significant asset in the practice of feng shui. This is because much of feng shui assessments are highly visual, requiring the human eye to make important evaluations with respect to shapes, terrain and contours.

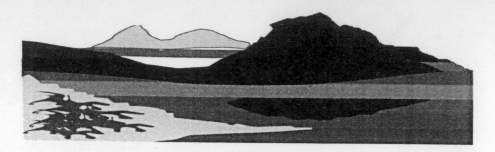

This dimension of feng shui practice has been collectively grouped under what is generally referred to as the Form or Landscape School of feng shui. Here the physical surroundings are judged according to how they visually appear. Mountains, hills, rivers, roads, levels, undulations, shape, smells, and just about everything that assails the senses, enter into the analysis of the surrounding environment. In addition, the quality of the soil, the strength of the winds, the intensity of the sunlight, the lushness of plants, and the angle of inclines, are factored into the feng shui man's evaluation of the land.

Literally translated, feng shui means wind water. Basically it is these two elements that have carved out the land resulting in the physical formations of the living earth. What feng shui offers are guidelines that enable the practitioner to interpret the features of the landscape in terms of whether they bring good or bad energy, and thus, whether they will bring auspicious or inauspicious luck to those who live in their vicinity.

The auspicious and inauspicious features of visual feng shui, as defined under the Form School, are very important to get right. The effect of bad landscape feng shui supersedes good compass feng shui. This is a vitally important first rule of feng shui practice to remember; that the physical structures of both the natural and man-made environment can destroy carefully worked out feng shui orientations.

Activating luck

Feng shui is also about consciously activating excellent luck in your environment and in your living space. Having learnt how to protect yourself, your home and your office from the incidence of bad feng shui (covered in Parts 2 and 3 in this book), the next step is to learn to energize the specific types of good fortune. These are covered in detail in Part 4.

This is an exciting aspect of feng shui practice. There is an impressive array of feng shui symbolism that can be effectively energized within corners of any home, room, or office, to create eight broad ranging types of luck. You can activate luck in your career and in your professional relationships. It is possible to improve your health, and enhance the luck for every member of your family. You can magnify luck for your children, and improve their luck for examinations. And, finally, you can create the kind of luck that enhances your income, bringing you wealth.

The promise of feng shui is thus exciting. What does it take to tap into these luck-bringing energies? It is not simply an understanding of the theory and philosophy of feng shui. It is also the need to start living in a state of awareness of the subtle changes in your environment. Get used to seeing your environment with feng shui eyes. Develop sensitivity to the powerful, yet invisible, energies surrounding you.

The trinity of luck

Understand from the start that feng shui is simply one component of the trinity of luck. Feng shui is earth luck in the trinity of heaven, earth and mankind luck – or tien ti ren, to use the Chinese words.

It is in this context that the trinity of luck exerts its influence on the results of feng shui practice. This explains that everyone has three types of luck:

◆ Heaven luck determines your fate and it is something over which you have no control; it determines the condition of your birth, your character and your circumstances. It is like karma.

◆ Earth luck comes from living in harmony with the environment and is encapsulated in the body of knowledge known as feng shui. Earth luck is within our control for we can choose whether or not we wish to live harmoniously with the energies of our living space.

◆ Mankind luck is the luck we create for ourselves and so it, too, is within our control. Good feng shui brings the opportunities for advancement and happiness to our doorstep, but whether or not we take advantage of these opportunities and maximize them to their fullest potential depends on us.

How, and at what speed this luck changes or magnifies, depends on how we are influenced by the trinity of luck and it is in this context that feng shui should be understood and practised. If your heaven luck is good, feng shui makes it better and this, when supplemented by your own efforts improves your circumstances, making you

The I Ching

By developing a practical attitude towards the practice of feng shui you will find it easier to understand the more advanced theories of feng shui which take account of the time dimension in the concept of luck. This time dimension reflects the more profound aspects of *I Ching* philosophy, upon which feng shui is based. The *I Ching*'s view of the Universe is that all things change; hence it is called *The Book of Changes*.

The *I Ching* says that in all good fortune there is the kernel of misfortune, which can rise and overwhelm, and become full-fledged misfortune. It also contends that in misfortune there is simultaneously the seed of great good fortune.

more comfortable. On the other hand, if your heaven luck is not so good, feng shui can at best only reduce your sufferings and problems. Good feng shui can make you comfortable. But it cannot make you a seriously wealthy person if that is not in your heaven luck.

Practising feng shui

Anyone can learn feng shui. It is not a difficult subject, either to understand or to practise. Feng shui is neither a spiritual nor a religious practice. It does not require an intensity of faith or possession of metaphysical or psychic abilities. Feng shui is a science, a method, a technique — it is based on a comprehensive set of guidelines that expresses the Chinese view of the Universe. It defines the existence of a life force in the natural environment, and this life force can be either auspicious or accommodating, or it can be threatening and lethal.

Feng shui advises the arrangement of one's personal space in a way that taps into the multitude of auspicious energies circulating in abundance in the environment. It advocates the avoidance of structures and arrangements that inadvertently change this auspicious energy into poisonous energy. Most feng shui masters possess enough knowledge to capture accommodating energy and deflect poisonous energy. If you observe and practice the information contained in this book, you too will be able to achieve this.

Some commonly asked questions about the practice of feng shui

Q: How does feng shui work?

A: Feng shui advocates living in harmony with the earth's environment and its energy lines so that what is created is an auspicious balancing of the forces of nature. Feng shui contends that the atmosphere is crowded with invisible but powerful energy lines – some of these lines are auspicious while others are pernicious. So these energy lines bring discord or harmony; health or sickness; prosperity or poverty. The practice of feng shui has to do with the clever harnessing and accumulating of energy lines that are auspicious – what the Chinese refer to as harnessing the Dragon's cosmic breath.

Q: Is it necessary or advisable to contact a feng shui master?

A: A great deal of feng shui can be learnt fairly easily, as this book sets out to explain. However, like any other profession or discipline, practical experience does improve performance. It is from this perspective that feng shui master practitioners are useful to consult. In recent years, however, inflation has caught up with the profession, and those who make a living by offering their feng shui knowledge as consultants – if they are any good – are so popular and so in demand that their fees have soared in tandem with the demand for their services.

Nevertheless, those masters who are genuinely knowledgeable and experienced really are worth their weight in gold. The problem these days is the proliferation of 'wannabe' self-styled feng shui masters whose knowledge of feng shui is both shallow and inadequate. I therefore urge those who have only recently become acquainted with feng shui to be careful about inviting strangers to violate the privacy of their homes. Far better to learn about feng shui yourself. It is not difficult; it can be fun and it is certainly more satisfying.

Q: Does feng shui require massive renovations?

A: Not at all! The clever feng shui practitioner will always be able to find the least expensive way of combating poison arrows, or of activating good feng shui. This is because there are so many dimensions to the practice that it is often NOT possible to get everything right. A huge dose of common sense should be factored into the practice. Often just a small and subtle change in your sitting or sleeping direction could make a difference to your luck. Feng shui changes do not need to be massive to work. Energy lines are subtle. Think of your television signal – a small shift in the antenna of your aerial is often sufficient to spoil or improve the picture that comes through the tube. Likewise feng shui.

Q: Does feng shui always work?

A: Yes. If you get it right, feng shui always improves your living and work condition. But feng shui is not a magic cure-all for every one of your problems. Remember that feng shui represents only one third of the trinity of luck. If you are not fated to become a big tycoon, feng shui may make you rich, but not seriously wealthy. That depends on your heaven luck. And if your home enjoys good feng shui you will find yourself becoming busier. You will be presented with opportunities to enhance your life or improve your income. You must create your own mankind luck by seizing these opportunities, and accepting your good fortune.

Q: Can I practise the form school and ignore the compass school altogether?

A: Yes indeed you can. You will also be able to avoid being hit by bad feng shui. But compass school feng shui takes you deeper and allows you to discover powerful methods of seriously enhancing your luck. I always advise my friends to take things one step at a time. Go slowly because it is better to get the basics correct first before trying to apply everything all at once. Besides, it is never possible to get feng shui 100 per cent right.

Q: How do I know which feng shui advice to follow?

A: There are many different schools of feng shui. But all authentic feng shui is based on the same concepts. There are some excellent books out there that are based on authentic feng shui principles, but there are also some that simply blow my mind! Perhaps I should say here that so-called clearing the energies by clapping your hands and ringing bells is NOT feng shui. The danger in trying to simplify or Westernize an ancient Chinese practice is that it can sometimes lead to some hilarious versions of feng shui. Also be wary of those who claim to have spent a few months with a feng shui master and immediately set up practice as a consultant.

I do urge the exercise of good judgment simply because not many feng shui masters would willingly part with their trade secrets, and certainly not to someone who spends only a few years (let alone a few months) with him. Anyone familiar with the student-master relationship of the Chinese tradition will know that it takes many, many years before a master will reveal the real secrets of his skill or kung fu. I am thus very sceptical of those who claim to be experts having spent only a couple of seasons with a feng shui master.

Q: Why has feng shui become so popular in the West?

A: The current popularity of feng shui in the West reflects growing awareness of the cultural and philosophical approach to the Universe that the Chinese traditional sciences conceptualize. Feng shui is only one of several wonderful sciences of the mind/body and the environment that are gaining popularity in the West. People are beginning to realize that there are alternative ways and methods of viewing the Universe, of understanding the way energy moves and works, and how these energies affect our well-being. It is from such a perspective that feng shui can be seen as an additional tool that can be studied to understand the spirituality of the human soul and the environment. Thus, for example, feng shui uses the language of symbols to read and create the energies of the immediate environment. This opens up new pathways to understanding the spirituality of space.

Q: Can I practice feng shui without the theory?

A: Simple feng shui can be easily applied, irrespective of whether or not you understand the theory behind feng shui. However, it is not always easy to understand all the meanings of the fundamentals on a first reading. Therefore, if you wish, in this book you can proceed straight to the later chapters for easy, illustrated, feng shui tips that you can apply immediately. But when you are unsure, or if the illustration does not exactly fit your situation, then having the theoretical concepts to refer to become vital. It is not necessary to instantly understand everything, but do try to think things through when you get confused.

PART 1

Feng shui essentials

Making a start

All feng shui practice revolves around a comprehensive understanding of nine main principles. These are the conceptual underpinnings that make up the foundation of feng shui knowledge and practice. When used together, however, these principles can sometimes lead to recommendations that may seem contradictory. In such instances, one should make a judgement on which particular tenet is more important for your particular circumstance.

This is why an experienced feng shui eye can be such an asset. When in doubt it is useful to remember that the physical form of the environment emits powerful energies, and that shar chi, the killing breath (see pages 52-3, when generated by a particularly fierce poison arrow, is capable of destroying all other carefully contrived placements, that may well have taken many of the principles into account. So before you go to the next stage of energizing to create good feng shui, make sure nothing is hurting the feng shui of your space. It is best to always take a defensive approach.

The condition and quality of your exterior feng shui is more important than the layout and decoration of your interiors. The effect of external structures, in a radius of about at least half a mile (kilometre), can threaten your family's well being, make your life barren, and wipe out all your opportunities to improve your life. The curve of a river, the bend of a road, the shape of a flyover, even the roof of your neighbour's house; these and a variety of other structures that are said to emit killing breath can, singly or together, destroy the harmony of any home if it is orientated in a threatening way. This happens when the front of your house, and especially the main door, directly faces a building, a structure or an object that is sending symbolic poison arrows towards your home. It is therefore of the utmost importance that the development of feng shui awareness begins with a complete scan of the environment that surrounds your home.

Look in front of you, behind you and even

Feng shui's nine main principles
1 The Pa Kua and Lo Shu Square
2 Finding auspicious land sites
3 Selecting and creating regular shapes
4 Energizing the five elements
5 Balancing yin and yang
6 The dragon's cosmic breath
7 Deflecting the killing breath
8 Using symbols and numbers
9 Formula feng shui.

Feng shui awareness

Learning to see with feng shui eyes means developing an awareness of the sights and smells of your environment; becoming aware of the levels of the land, and the way topography curves, rises and falls. It means developing an appreciation for the winds and waters that surround you. It means taking note of changes within your environment. Be sensitive to the presence of new buildings, new roads, and new developments. Most important, always relate anything new in your environment to how your house, and your space, is affected.

look above you. The buildings and structures that are in front of you have the greatest potential to be damaging to your feng shui. Behind, it is the lack of land, structures and buildings that cause bad feng shui. Above you, if you lie in the path of planes, the daily noise and disturbance creates turbulence and is therefore also seen to be bad feng shui.

If you are looking for a new home, it is a good idea to investigate the neighbourhood before buying. Look out for all the signs of good feng shui – that the roads and pavements are clean, plants are thriving, the grass grows green, flowers bloom, homes are well maintained. You should be looking for an overall air of prosperity and happiness. Places of bad feng shui always look run down and dilapidated. Corrupt energy brings down the luck of the residents causing the downward spiral to get worse and worse. There is an air of sadness.

The Pa Kua and Lo Shu square

The practice of feng shui is believed to have started four thousand years ago although this, in many ways, is conjecture. Feng shui's origins can be traced to the influence of the *I Ching*, China's greatest classic. The *I Ching* is the source book of much of the traditions and cultural practice of the Chinese. The *I Ching*'s origins are still being traced by scholars, to an age and time that could well take us even further back into antiquity.

Thus, the most important tools of feng shui analysis which have survived the centuries, offer exciting similarities to other branches of Chinese traditional practice. Perhaps the most important of these are the eight trigrams – these are sets of three broken and/or unbroken lines that make up the root of the *I Ching*'s magnificent set of 64 hexagrams. These eight trigrams are arranged around an eight-sided shape called the Pa Kua, and the way they are placed is the essence of the feng shui principles.

There are two arrangements of these trigrams around the Pa Kua, and in the old days when the practice of feng shui focused on both the houses of the living and also on the houses of the dead, both arrangements were used in analysis.

Yin feng shui

The Early Heaven Arrangement of the trigrams around the Pa Kua was used when the feng shui of tombs and burial grounds was being undertaken. Indeed, the Chinese believed that this branch of feng shui (called yin feng shui), was extremely potent, and was far more powerful in its long ranging effects on a family's fortunes than any other type of feng shui. Some still say that yin feng shui lasts through at least five generations.

The most colourful evidence of the application of yin feng shui can be seen in the orientation of the Ming Tombs located just outside Beijing. The Chinese also tell stories that describe the auspicious orientation of ancestors' graves that led to the rise of latter day emperors like Mao Tse Tung and Deng Xiao Ping.

Yin Pa Kua in the home

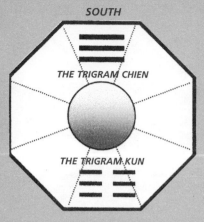

SOUTH

THE TRIGRAM CHIEN

THE TRIGRAM KUN

THE YIN PA KUA.

I strongly urge everyone who has been advised to use the Yin Pa Kua to deflect poison arrows to make sure that you do *not* hang it anywhere *inside* your home or office. This Pa Kua gives off killing energy that causes severe bad luck. It should only ever be hung outside and never inside the house. Even for the outside, you should endeavour to use other feng shui corrective methods if you are aiming them at your neighbours. Always try to use corrective measures that do not hurt others.

Today, yin feng shui is fast disappearing as many of the old masters refrain from undertaking assignments that involve the design of tombs and grave sites. In Taiwan, Hong Kong, Malaysia and Singapore, however, there continues to be a small group of tycoons who have already earmarked their burial sites and who have arranged to have their yin feng shui done. For most of the ordinary population, though, yin feng shui is deemed impractical. It is easier to be cremated, since cremation does not cause good or bad feng shui.

In the yin Pa Kua, the trigram chien is placed in the south directly opposite the kun trigram that is placed in the north. This Early Heaven Arrangement of the trigrams is believed to make the Pa Kua a potent symbol of protection. It is this arrangement that those who sell feng shui paraphernalia draw onto protective Pa Kuas, and which are hung outside doorways to deflect hostile shar chi caused by obstacles, straight roads and other offensive structures.

Yang feng shui

Yang feng shui applies only to the houses of the living, and the Pa Kua relied upon for analysis is the Later Heaven Arrangement, or yang Pa Kua, where the arrangement of the trigrams differs considerably from the yin Pa Kua. The amateur practitioner should learn to tell the difference between these two Pa Kuas. An easy way of differentiating is to note where the main trigrams chien and kun are located.

In the yang Pa Kua, the trigram chien is placed in the northwest while the trigram kun is placed in the southwest. Thus, in the feng shui of houses of the living, the place of the patriarch is the northwest, and this orientation or corner of the house becomes a very important one. It should therefore not contain the toilet, kitchen or store room. In the same way, the place of the matriarch is the southwest and, likewise, this corner of the home should not house the toilet.

In the practice of yang feng shui it is important that the correct Pa Kua be used to undertake the analysis, since almost all of the feng shui recommendations relate to directions, orientations, and elements based on the yang arrangement of the eight trigrams. This is a fundamental underpinning of feng shui theory.

The lo shu turtle

A second major symbol suggestive of feng shui antiquity is the nine sector Lo Shu square that is popularly associated with the celestial turtle. Legend has it that four thousand years ago a celestial turtle emerged from the waters of the river Lo bearing on its back an arrangement of numbers that provided the key to unlocking the secrets of the Pa Kua. This arrangement of the numbers 1 to 9 around a nine-sector grid or square is the basis of much of what is sometimes referred to as feng shui magic or, more accurately, formula feng shui.

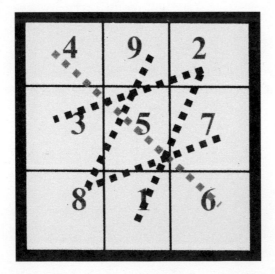

The back of the turtle carried the symbols of the Lo Shu numbers.

There are scholars who have discovered that the flow of the numbers around the Lo Shu forms a symbol which closely resembles important signs in Indian astrology, and, in fact, looks exactly like the sigil of the planet Saturn in Hebrew mythology. This symbol is shown in the illustration below (in dotted lines). Note the flow of the numbers 1 to 9 that create this \symbol.

The Lo Shu arrangement of numbers with dotted lines showing the flow of numbers 1 to 9 that create this symbol.

Finding auspicious
land sites

The practice of feng shui always starts with the search for auspicious locations. In older days, a good location was everything, and natural contours such as hills and streams featured prominently in the feng shui expert's list of things to consider. Today, man-made structures like roads, buildings, and entire townships and cities, bring new dimensions to the practice of feng shui. As a result, analysis of the natural landscape must now be supplemented by analysis of steel and concrete buildings, as well as roads, flyovers and highways.

Green dragon white tiger

Before going any further, it is necessary to understand the importance of the terms green tiger and white tiger as they are intrinsic to the understanding of what makes a site auspicious. In Hong Kong, the term 'green dragon white tiger' is synonymous with feng shui. What is referred to here is the symbolism of the four celestial creatures that represent the fundamental foundation of feng shui theory. These four creatures are the black turtle, crimson phoenix, green dragon and the white tiger. They define the parameters of classical feng shui.

The black turtle

Behind, or in the north, is the place of the black turtle which offers the luck of support. If this hill is lacking, your feng shui is incomplete and the luck that protects you and your family from generation to generation will be missing. The black turtle hills are most crucial, especially to the patriarch or breadwinner of the family. In fact, the turtle is such a powerful symbol that families who rear any species of this celestial creature – the tortoise or the terrapin – often find family fortunes steadily improving as the years pass. The turtle brings slow and steady improvement, enhancing fortunes and lifestyles. In my thirty years of observation I have never seen this turtle feng shui tip fail.

The crimson phoenix

The place of the crimson phoenix, which brings you the luck
of opportunities, is in front of your home directly facing your
front door, or in the south. If your front door faces south, it
is an excellent orientation for attracting this kind of luck.
According to ancient Chinese legend, the phoenix is the
mythical king of all feathered creatures. It is said to appear
every thousand years, and only at a time when a great and benevolent
emperor rules the land. The phoenix thus appears during auspicious times.
The phoenix is also revered for its magnificent come-back qualities. From
the earth, the ashes of broken dreams and despair, the phoenix rises,
stunning and magnificent, to try again and to achieve success. In this way,
the phoenix is said to symbolize success in the face of defeat, and help from
unexpected quarters. In feng shui, this refers to a little hillock which can
also symbolize a footstool to rest your weary legs! Should it be missing, the
phoenix hillock is usually easy to create by building a small mound of earth
that is, say, about 1 m (3 ft) high. Any feathered bird can symbolize the
pheonix, including roosters, flamingoes and peacocks.

The green dragon

On the left side of your main door as you look out from your
home, and better still if this also corresponds to the east
orientation of your home (since the dragon is then deemed to
be in his own element), is the place of the auspicious green
dragon. This creature brings the luck of every kind of
material success – wealth, position, influence and power. The
dragon is regarded as the ultimate symbol of good fortune, and is the
most important celestial creature in the Chinese pantheon of legendary
creatures. In feng shui, the side that represents the green dragon hills should
be slightly more elevated than the right-hand side. This allows the influence
of the dragon to be dominant in your personal environment.

The white tiger

On the right-hand side of the main door, and it
would be ideal if this corresponded to the west
orientation of the home, is the place of the white
tiger, which offers the luck of protection. In feng
shui, it is believed that the white tiger is present only
in places where the green dragon exists. So, in terms of

The best sites

The mountain behind this house represents the protective turtle and the hill on the left represents the green dragon.

The most auspicious type of land is undulating, where the slopes are gentle, where there are hills and valleys, where there is a good mix of sunlight and shade and where the winds do not blow too strong. In such places, look for the patches of land where grass grows luscious and there is a flow of water. These are the places that house the dragon, and so are auspicious.

hill formations, if you cannot find hills that resemble or symbolize the dragon, the tiger is deemed to be missing. The protection of the white tiger guards the family from being robbed, hurt or defeated. The luck of the white tiger must not be underestimated.

But it is vital to make certain the ferocity of the tiger is never aroused or turned against the residents. This means that the ground level on the right-hand side of the home or garden should be slightly lower than that of the left, allowing the dragon to stay dominant, thereby keeping the tiger under control. If the land on the tiger side is higher than the land on the dragon side, feng shui corrections will have to be introduced to diffuse the white tiger. In this connection, I always warn against placing pictures of the tiger inside the house. Unless you are born in the lunar year of either dragons or tigers (see pages 72–4), not everyone can bear the fierce energy of the tiger presence.

Overcoming inauspicious orientation

As feng shui in its broadest perspective is the study of environments, knowledge of feng shui shows you how to position your home to draw on the luck of each of the four celestial animals. Once you understand the major guidelines, you will be able to orientate your house or building in a way

Land that is completely flat is not auspicious; introduce elevations to the land to improve its feng shui luck.

which taps into the land's auspicious energy, and ensure that your house or building blends harmoniously with this energy. Often, this calls for nothing more serious than to relocate or re-orientate your main door. Should this not be possible and your home is suffering from an inauspicious orientation, corrective feng shui offers methods of installing features that help negate the bad features, or to block off the bad views.

In the country, start by looking for the green dragon. This describes places where the contours are undulating, and there are hills as well as valleys. Land that is flat does not have the dragon – there is no place there to build a dragon's lair. Flat land is therefore regarded as inauspicious – its energy is far too yin. In the old days, such land would have been rejected outright. In today's modern, anything-is-possible approach, however, such land can be made auspicious by the artificial introduction and careful placement of boulders, hillocks, tall buildings and other structures that bring in a healthy dose of yang energy. This symbolically creates the dragon, and consequently transforms an inauspicious location into one that is lucky and vibrant with yang energy.

Land whose terrain is too steep, with hills that rise sharply, resembling tongues of fire, is also deemed inauspicious. These are places where surrounding hills will belong to the fire element (see page 43), and places like these also cannot house dragons, being entirely too yang. In the hands of a clever developer, however, fire hills can be reshaped, and flattened and the valleys filled, thereby creating a far more conducive environment, one that could well attract the dragon. Likewise, artificial waterways that have been added in strategic places could well enhance the much needed yin energy. As a result, once again through man's intervention, an unlucky location can be transformed into an auspicious one.

Land that is too steep is also inauspicious. The terrain is too yang.

The important rules in landscape feng shui

The mountain must be behind

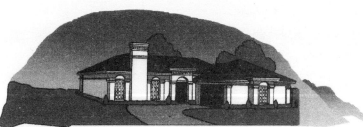

Right: Land on the left is higher than land on the right.

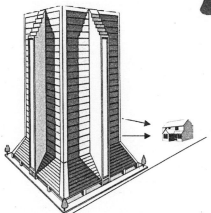

Above: This house here does not even have a chance against this huge building directly in front of it. There cannot be any good luck for the residents. The solution is to close the main door and use the back door instead, thereby turning the building into a protective mountain.

Below: Water near your home is best if it is in full view of the front door.

This means that your home, or the building that houses your home (if you live in an apartment), should be orientated so that the main front door or the gate entering the house does not confront the mountain. If your main door opens directly to a mountain, your feng shui is regarded as enormously bad. This is described as confrontational.

In the city, a high wall or a large building is like a mountain. If your main entrance is facing such a structure, think seriously about re-orientating your door so that the large structure is then behind you rather than in front. Let your back door open to the mountain. In this way you will be tapping into its protective energies. Remember that when you 'confront' the mountain, you will always lose.

Water in the front of your home

Any water in the vicinity of your home should be in front of it and it must be in full view of the front door. When I refer to water, I mean the natural flow of water such as in a river. A nearby waterway passing behind your home indicates opportunities that are just out of reach and you will not be able to take advantage of those apparently coming your way. Deals and promises, which you think are in the bag, could slip away, too.

A river should flow past the main door.

Five types of mountains

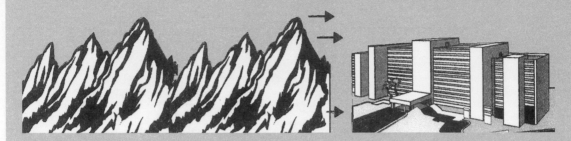

When looking at the hills and mountains that surround your land, or which surround a city, it is useful to understand the feng shui meanings that are associated with their shape. To the Chinese, mountains have always been desirable places to live because they believe elevated land forms are the natural habitat of the auspicious earth dragons.

Hills and mountains can be classified into five types of shapes that coincide with each of the five elements, water, fire, metal, wood and earth (see pages 42-3). The classification is based on their profile when viewed from the horizon and takes account of the shape of their summits and the steepness of their slopes. The significance of the mountain shape directly relates to their desirability as places to live.

The amateur practitioner of feng shui will definitely have difficulty identifying the different types of hills, but don't worry about this. Once you know the basic differences, the

Above: Sharply ridge slopes are regarded as inauspicious and it is best not to have your home pointing directly at such mountains.

feng shui eye will develop with experience. Bear in mind, however, that different shapes usually occur together and these combinations have feng shui implications that can require the experienced eye of a feng shui master to interpret. The essential thing to remember is that undulating, gentle slopes are always auspicious, while sharply ridged slopes are not. Indeed, slopes that appear sharp and ridged are likened to poison arrows. If such a ridge is pointed at your home or building, it is considered a deadly arrow.

From a feng shui viewpoint, the three types of mountain shapes that are deemed prosperous are the shapes that correspond to the wood, earth and metal elements. Ridged hill shapes are of the water element and are regarded as too yin and, generally, conical

Above: Water element mountains.

Below: Fire element mountains.

shaped mountains are of the fire element and are considered too yang. Both types of mountains are not considered auspicious unless your birth date is in harmony with the fire and water elements (see pages 72-4).

Wood shaped hills are generally round and high. This type of mountain is associated with the wealth planet Jupiter. The wood element is also suggestive of growth. People

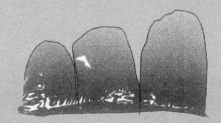

Wood shaped hills enhance wealth luck.

born in the year of the fire element (see pages 72-4) will benefit hugely if they live in the vicinity of mountains that are shaped like this. Mountains like these also have the potential of housing dragons and so are auspicious.

Square shaped earth element mountains.

Earth element mountains are generally square. They look like plateaux with a flat, extensive summit. The planet associated with this mountain is Saturn. People born in the years of the metal element (see page s 72-4) are particularly suited to mountains that have this characteristic shape.

Metal element mountains are extremely auspicious.

Metal element mountains are softly rounded and oblong. The base of such mountains is broad so that the effect is one of undulating elevations. This type of mountain is suggestive of gold and is considered to be very prosperous.

Left: If land on your right-hand side (the tiger side) is higher, erect a tall bright light on your dragon side to raise the energy, thereby correcting the balance.

Land levels

Land level on the left-hand side of your house should be higher than land on the right-hand side. The dragon (on the left) must dominate the tiger (on the right) for the feng shui to be auspicious. In the event that the tiger side is higher, one good way of correcting the situation would be to erect a very tall light on the left, or dragon, side. This serves to raise the chi of the dragon side, creating much needed balance. Another solution is to artificially change the contours by creating a small hill on the left-hand side, if this is possible.

If you live in the city, this guideline would be reflected by the presence of a slightly taller building on the left side of your building. However, make certain that your building does not appear to be hemmed in. It is inauspicious if buildings are too close to you.

If yours is the centre building, then the building on your left represents the green dragon. If it is slightly higher than your building it is an auspicious feature. Meanwhile, if the building on your right is slightly lower than the building on your left, the perfect white tiger

Below: The building to the left of a building symbolizes the green dragon; and the building to the right is the white tiger. The green dragon should be taller than the white tiger.

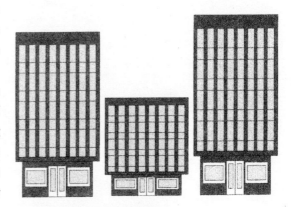

Water on mountain

Water on mountain is one of the four major warnings of feng shui. When water reaches its zenith, it overflows, causing grave misfortune. Thus houses should never have blue coloured roofing tiles. The blue suggests the water element, and this alone can be enough to sometimes cause severe financial losses.

symbol has been created, and your building is considered to have auspicious classical feng shui. If the centre building is also not dwarfed by either of the buildings beside it, the feng shui is not affected in any negative way.

Home on the hillside

It is important to know which part of the hill is more auspicious. In Hong Kong, the local business community, especially the very wealthy, live on the hill slopes of the island. Those who know, do not live at the bottom nor at the very top of the hill, known as the peak. Instead, the Chinese prefer to live in apartments and houses that are located at mid-levels. They know that the most auspicious part of the hill is in the middle, where they can enjoy both the view of the sea as well as the protection of the peak high behind them. The least desirable part of the hill is at the summit, especially if it is above the fog line. According to feng shui guidelines, living at the summit of a hill exposes you to fierce winds. There is no protection and no support.

The same rationale applies to living at the penthouse level of high rise buildings. It is perfectly fine to live on the top floor if your apartment block is not the highest, but I would advise you not to be at the summit of a cluster of high rise buildings. The danger of being at the very top is seriously compounded if there is also a presence of water. Penthouse or hilltop estates, which have large swimming pools, are particularly vulnerable.

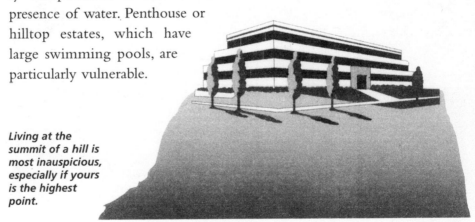

Living at the summit of a hill is most inauspicious, especially if yours is the highest point.

Selecting and creating regular shapes

The next important principle that is essential to good feng shui is the regularity of the shape of land sites, buildings and other structures. This rule encompasses the philosophy of completeness and symmetry. Completeness suggests that structures and shapes should not have any corners or sectors missing. Symmetry implies there should be balance so that no single element or type of energy should be overly dominant.

In feng shui, therefore, outlines that result in unbalanced shapes are considered inauspicious. This principle is applicable to land plots, buildings, rooms, and furniture. Examples of auspicious shapes are all regular, while inauspicious shapes usually have missing corners, and are irregular.

Examples of auspicious shapes

These may be viewed as two- or three-dimensional shapes and vertically or horizontally, or from all elevations.

Below: Some auspicious shapes. Note the balance of each outline.

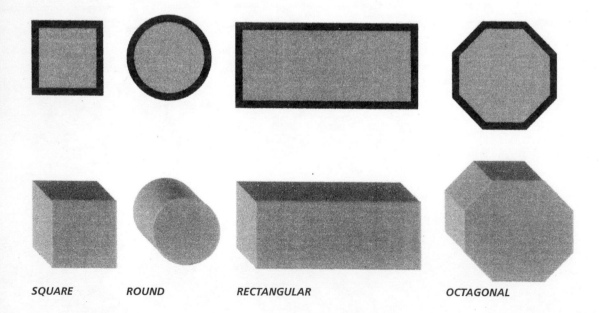

SQUARE   **ROUND**   **RECTANGULAR**   **OCTAGONAL**

Examples of inauspicious shapes

Viewed from various elevations, these shapes tend to have missing corners or irregular lines and curves. Triangular shapes are considered inauspicious. If the building resembles an inauspicious object, like a knife for instance, then the location of the main door becomes crucial in determining the overall luck of the house.

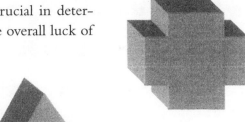
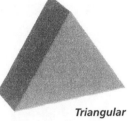

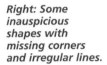
Right: Some inauspicious shapes with missing corners and irregular lines.

Triangular   *Cross-shaped*   *Unbalanced*

The problem of missing corners

Regular shapes are luckier than irregular shapes because the latter creates the phenomena of missing corners. Usually this creates imbalance. Missing corners detract from the luck of the particular corner that is missing, the severity of which is determined by the occupant's attitude towards life.

Missing corners are easy to determine when the shape of the house can be formed into a four-cornered rectangle as shown in the first three examples below. By superimposing a rectangle over the layout and regularizing the shape of the house, missing corners become obvious.

The way to correct these missing corners is to build extensions to cover the area (or areas) in question in order to regularize the shape. A second method is to place a tall light in the corners as indicated by the dots.

An L-shaped house   *A U-shaped house*   *A Z-shaped house*

Simple missing corners that are easy to detect.

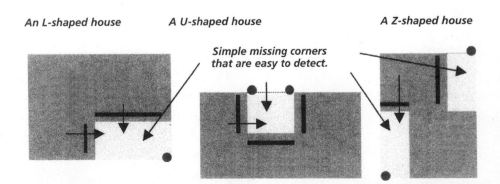

In the U-shaped house illustrated at the foot of the previous page, the lights can flank the entrance into the heart of the home, as shown. It is also possible to use a wall mirror to visually extend a wall. This method can be used only if the mirror does not reflect the main door, a staircase or a toilet.

Protruding corners

In the same way that corners are deemed to be missing, houses may also have protruding corners. Where there is a protrusion, it is said the energy of the corner is strengthened. Examples of protruding corners are shown in the illustrations below.

How lucky or unlucky the missing and protruding corners are for your home, and which member of the family gets most affected by this enhanced good or bad luck, can be determined by feng shui analysis.

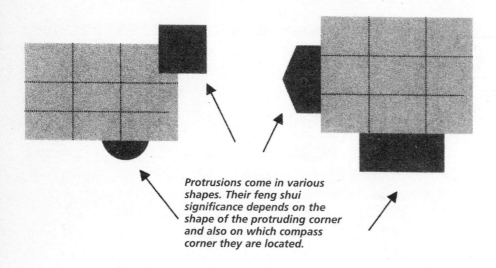

Protrusions come in various shapes. Their feng shui significance depends on the shape of the protruding corner and also on which compass corner they are located.

Identifying the different areas of your home

First, invest in a good compass, although it does not have to be a very complicated one. Get a boy scout compass or an outdoor compass from a hardware store. It is not necessary to use a Chinese compass nor should you flip the directions around. Every direction referred to in this book corresponds to the direction read off any Western style compass.

To identify the different areas of your home, take the compass direc-

Determining the difference between missing and protruding corners

The south affects the reputation and popularity of residents

The southeast represents wealth luck. If this corner is missing incomes become reduced

A missing southwest corner adversely affects marriage and love relationships

The east affects health luck

In the west, the luck of the children get affected

The northeast affects study luck

The northwest represents help from important people

SOUTHEAST CORNER	SOUTH CORNER	SOUTHWEST CORNER
EAST CORNER	CENTRE	WEST CORNER
NORTHEAST CORNER	NORTH CORNER	NORTHWEST CORNER

North affects career luck

The simplest way to identify missing areas or protruding corners is to use the rectangle or square as the basic shape, which represents the complete, or whole, space. When this shape is superimposed on a two-dimensional layout drawing of your home, apartment or office, you will be able to see immediately whether you have a missing corner or a protruding corner. For example, an L-shaped layout has a missing corner, while bay windows and annexes often represent protruding corners.

A missing corner detracts from the luck of the corner that is missing, while a protruding one strengthens the luck of that corner. The kind of luck that is affected depends on where the corner is located, ie in which compass sector (see illustration, above).

tion from the centre of the house, and identify each grid of the Lo Shu square by superimposing a nine sector grid onto a ground floor plan of the house. Be as accurate as possible when taking measurements and compass directions.

Once you have superimposed a square or rectangular grid over your home's plan, by reading off the compass you will be able to identify each direction and corresponding area of the grid. Where the needle points to north, the grid lying in that direction represents the north. Superimposing the square onto the plan allows you to identify two things:

◆ Which direction each of the other grids represent. In this way, once you have noted all the eight directions you would have identified each sector of your home. You can then proceed to do feng shui analysis based on the compass sectors. Remember that this same method can be repeated in each room to identify the north, south, east or west corners.

◆ It also allows you to note the dividing lines between the sectors. These lines are imaginary but because you are using the Lo Shu square to divide your house or room into nine equal sectors, you are in effect using the Lo Shu to establish the compass perimeters of your home. Try to be as accurate as you can.

Protruding corners and the elements

You can use element analysis to determine whether the shape of a protruding corner is lucky or unlucky. Establish which element the shape represents (see below) and how it combines with the element of the corner it occupies. If the elements are in harmony, ie productive, the luck is good. If the elements clash, then the luck is inauspicious.

Square shapes

These belong to the earth element. This is a shape that enhances anything which represents the metal element. Square protrusions are excellent in the northwest and west corners. They also bring good luck when placed in the southwest and the northeast corners. They bring bad luck when placed in the north corner, or if the main door is located in the north corner. This is due to the destructive relationship between earth and the water element of the north.

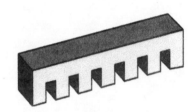

Square protrusions.

Round or semi-circular shapes

These belong to the metal element. Protruding structures of this shape will enhance the north, northwest and west corners of a house, or if the main doors are located in these corners. Round protrusions, however, can bring bad luck to the east and southeast corners, or if the main door is placed in those corners. This is because metal is said to destroy the wood element of the east and southeast.

Round or semi-circular protrusions.

Rectangular shapes

Protrusions with this shape are said to belong to the wood element. They bring auspicious luck if placed in the southeast,

Rectangular protrusions.

east and south corners, or when the main door is located in those sectors. They are said to cause luck to diminish if located in the southwest or northeast. Wood is said to destroy south.

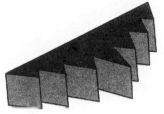

Triangular shaped protrusions.

Triangular-shaped protruding corners

These belong to the fire element, and are auspicious when placed in the south. They are also excellent for the southwest and the northeast corners but are said to cause a loss of luck when placed in the northwest and west corners. Triangular-shaped protrusions come in several different versions as shown to the left.

Wavy shaped protrusions.

Wavy-shaped protrusions

As shown in the illustration to the left, wavy-shaped protrusions are said to be of the water element and are auspicious when placed north, east or southeast. They are harmful when placed in the south.

Other lucky and unlucky shapes

In addition to looking at the regularity of the shape, and applying element symbolism, feng shui experts use other methods for determining the luck of

Lucky shapes based on Chinese characters

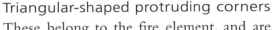

The shape on the left resembles the word ji, meaning luck, while the shape on the right resembles wang, meaning king. Both shapes are considered auspicious.

Unlucky shapes based on Chinese characters

The shape on the left resembles the word xia, meaning down, while the shape on the right resembles xiong, meaning bad luck. Both shapes are regarded as most inauspicious.

Steps are regarded with some suspicion, and buildings that have their belly missing are said to symbolize extreme bad luck.

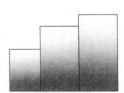

There are mixed opinions on the steps effect.
The missing belly effect is definitely bad feng shui.

shapes. A popular way of gauging the luck of buildings, for instance, is to see what Chinese character, if any, the building resembles. Here are some examples of shapes which can be viewed either by looking at a building's elevation or its layout, ie seen from above:

Family members and missing or protruding corners

The member of the family who gets most affected by a missing or enhanced corner is analysed according to the placement of the trigrams around the compass directions based on the Later Heaven Arrangement of trigrams (see below).

The most serious missing corner is usually the northwest since this affects the luck of the patriarch of the house, especially serious if he is also the breadwinner. A protruding corner here is thus more desirable than a missing corner. If, on the other hand, the breadwinner is the matriarch, then it is the southwest that becomes the corner to enhance with a protrusion. Certain feng shui experts contend that placing the main door in this corner also benefits the matriarch.

Auspicious and inauspicious directions of each member of the family should also be calculated based on the Pa Kua Lo Shu formula. This formula spells out auspicious or inauspicious corners for individuals based on their dates of birth. This compass formula, which divides people into west group or east group people, is given on pages 72-6. If the corner is said

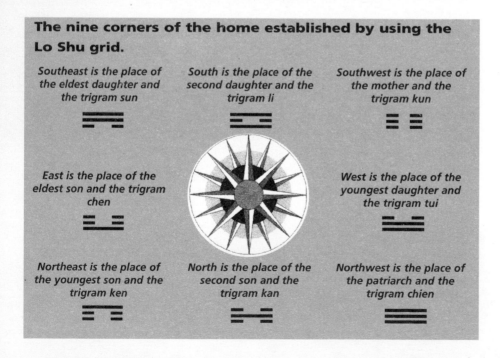

The nine corners of the home established by using the Lo Shu grid.

Southeast is the place of the eldest daughter and the trigram sun

South is the place of the second daughter and the trigram li

Southwest is the place of the mother and the trigram kun

East is the place of the eldest son and the trigram chen

West is the place of the youngest daughter and the trigram tui

Northeast is the place of the youngest son and the trigram ken

North is the place of the second son and the trigram kan

Northwest is the place of the patriarch and the trigram chien

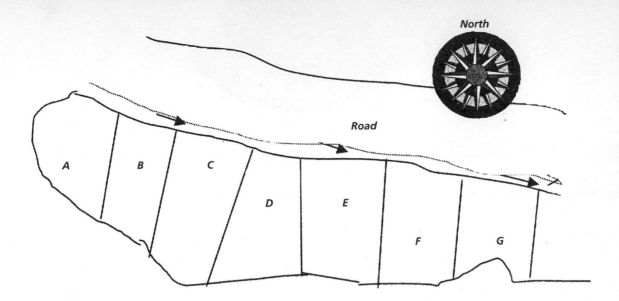

to be auspicious for you based on the formula, then generally a missing corner detracts from your luck, while an extension of that corner strengthens your luck.

Choosing a plot of land

Shapes in feng shui, whether rooms, building or land plots, take on significance when seen from the air or when viewed in layout view. When selecting sites go for those that are regular, as square as possible, and deep rather than wide. Note the land plots above, each of which seem to be fairly regular on first looking at them.

Plot A has a protruding corner on the west side.

Plot C has a protruding corner at the back while plot G has a missing corner. Plot C also has a wide entrance and is narrow at the back and some feng shui experts interpret this as having an inability to save money.

Plot D has a small mouth and a large back, and this type of land shape is said to resemble a money bag, with obvious favourable connotations.

Plots E and F are the most regular and so the most favourable.

While the shape of land sites is important, it is also advisable to take orientations as this will indicate the range of directions available for your house orientation. Also investigate the way the contours of the surroundings affect your land. In the example shown, the land is higher on the west than on the east side since the water is flowing from west to east (see dotted line). This will have different implications for each piece of land, and for each house that ultimately gets built.

Energizing the five elements

The theory of the five elements is basic to all branches of Chinese divinitive practice. From astrological fortune telling to oracle forecasting, understanding the productive and destructive cycles of the five elements – how they interact with each other to create positive auspicious energy or negative inauspicious energy – is what offers potency to the practice.

In feng shui, the attributes of the elements influence each of the eight sectors of the compass. The four cardinal and four secondary directions each have a corresponding element. So the easiest method of creating good feng shui is simply to energize the element of each compass sector. Understanding element attributes is thus essential.

In addition to compass directions, feng shui also contends that everything in the Universe possesses intangible energies that have element connotations. Seasons, colours, shapes, directions of energy flows and even numbers have their element equivalents. Their attributes and associations should be committed to memory because applications of element theory lie behind many of the feng shui diagnoses offered and feng shui cures suggested in this book. A number of feng shui enhancing techniques also have their roots in the five elements, which in Chinese are termed wu xing.

The use of element therapy in feng shui is very effective. But it is subtle and the amount of any element represented adds to the fine balance. Never forget that feng shui is about balance and harmony, and that excess of any single element is inauspicious. Too much water always drowns, and too much fire burns, irrespective of anything else.

The five elements

In using the elements in feng shui, it is necessary to be very subtle. In addition to the amounts and size of the elements represented, various other factors need to be considered. The time of year, the season, the colours of the room, the shapes that surrounds the space. Feng shui analysis should always encompass the entire package.

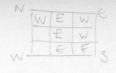

Fire

The ultimate yang element. It is an extremely powerful element but it does not exist of itself. It has to be created. Unlike the other elements, fire cannot be stored. Fire energy offers success in public life, brings fame, recognition and shining attainment to those who successfully activate its energies. But fire must also be kept under control at all times. An excess of fire energy can be fatal. Fire is associated with the south.

A fireplace in the south emphasizes the fire element of the south.

Water

The wealth energy in feng shui. Like fire, it is an extremely powerful element which can go out of control. Water energy moves downward, so when it overflows, it creates destruction and loss. Water energy brings prosperity. If you energize it correctly and in proper alignments with the other energies so that there is auspicious balance, water energy will make you rich beyond your expectations. Water is identified with the north.

Placed in the north, the water motif brings auspicious luck for careers.

Earth

The grounding energy, and it epitomizes the heart of feng shui. Tapping earth luck brings harmony and great family happiness, usually associated with the efforts of the matriarch. Earth is the element that dominates the southwest, the northeast and the centre grid of a home.

There is no better symbol of earth than the globe. Placed in the earth corners it activates excellent good luck.

Wood

This energy brings growth, expansion and advancement. Wood is the direction of the east and the southeast. Its energies bring the luck of material success. Like the branches of a tree, good luck grows ever increasingly outwards - wood being the only element which has life. Wood energy also confers excellent descendants' luck on families, and is especially beneficial to the sons of the family.

Wood can be represented by the trunk of a tree.

Metal

This energy brings the luck of powerful and helpful people, what the Chinese term heaven men. Metal is the element of the west and the northwest. It symbolizes the strength of heaven and the power of the patriarch. Metal is always associated with gold and silver, and its energy is dense and inward flowing. If you successfully tap into the auspicious metal energy, your life is one of power and great influence. If you wish to energize the luck of helpful people, one of the most potent methods is to hang a tiny golden bell in the northwest corner of your home.

Placed in the northwest, a golden bell brings immense good luck.

Other attributes of the five elements

Use these additional attributes for further analysis and creativity in practice.

	WOOD	WATER	FIRE	METAL	EARTH
Season	spring	winter	summer	autumn	between
Direction	east/SE	north	south	west/NW	SW/NE
Colour	green	blue/black	red	white	ochre
Shape	rectangle	wavy	triangular	round	square
Energy	outwards	descending	upwards	inwards	sideways
Numbers	3, 4	1	9	6, 7	2, 5, 8

Matching elements to the corners of the house

The best way to use element theory to enhance the feng shui of any home or room is to first identify the corners of the house or room. The exercise can be undertaken for the whole house, or it can be done individually for separate rooms. It can also apply to a desktop or table. Application of feng shui methods depend on how you demarcate your space. Thus, when we refer to, say, the south, this can mean the south wall of your room, your house, your land, your city or your country. The effect grows outwards in ever widening circles. This is because feng shui recognizes that any direction has no meaning except in relation to another direction.

An easy way of applying element therapy on your home is by using the correct colours and combination of colours for the different corners

---

Energizing the elements

THE SOUTHEAST Energize with wood	THE SOUTH Energize with fire	THE SOUTHWEST Energize with earth
THE EAST Energize with wood		THE WEST Energize with metal
THE NORTHEAST Energize with earth	THE NORTH Energize with water	THE NORTHWEST Energize with metal

---

and rooms. So red, or any shade of red, would be a good colour to use for curtains placed on windows located in the south part of the house or on the south wall of a particular room. This principle applies equally to carpets, covers, pillow cases and wallpaper. Using the same analogy, check against the table opposite to find the corresponding colours for the other corners, and incorporate these guidelines in your interior designs.

Energizing the luck of the corner can also be achieved by placing objects that symbolize the correct element. For example, energize the south with a fireplace, the southwest with a crystal; west with a horseshoe; north-west with a wind chime; north with a bowl of water; northeast with a ceramic pot; and the southeast and east with a pot plant. These objects are only suggestions; they are the ones I use with great success.

The interactive cycle of the elements

The energies of the elements do not stay static. They continuously interact with other objects within the environment. These objects emit energies of all five elements. The interaction of elements in the atmosphere is thus dynamic and constantly changing. Some of the elements relate productive-ly, and therefore favourably, with each other – creating the productive cycle. Others interact unfavourably, creating the destructive cycle.

When applying element analysis to the environment for feng shui purposes, it is vital that these harmonious and discordant cycles be noted. Their effect can be felt in colour combinations placed throughout the corners of rooms, in the use of materials and their mix, and in the design of shapes and lines for layout and interior decoration purposes.

Colour combinations

There are auspicious and inauspicious colour combinations. Here are some of the inauspicious combinations:

   Red/blue or red/black (very bad in a south corner)
   Red/metallic (very bad in a west or northwest corner)
   Green/yellow (extra harmful in the southwest and northeast)
   Yellow/blue (extra bad in the north)
   Green/metallic (extra bad in the east and southeast).

And here are some of the auspicious combinations:

   Green/red (excellent in the south, good in the east and southeast during the winter months)
   Red/yellow (excellent in the southwest and the northeast)

Yellow/metallic (excellent in the west and northwest)
Metallic/blue (excellent for the north)
Blue/green (excellent in the east and southeast).

Shape combinations

The auspicious combinations are:

1 Triangle added to square in the southwest and northeast
2 Square added to round in the northwest and west
3 Rectangle added to triangle in the south
4 Wavy added to rectangle in the southeast and east.

The productive cycle of the elements

This cycle of the elements shows a never ending cycle of production. It is an harmonious interaction, which is favourable for attracting the auspicious sheng chi (see pages 51–2). One element produces another in a circular flow of energy. This is the kind of harmony that we should endeavour to create in our living space.

From the productive cycle, the following attributes of elements can be applied for feng shui purposes:

Water is good for Wood, but Wood exhausts Water
Wood is good for Fire, but Fire exhausts Wood
Fire is good for Earth, but Earth exhausts Fire
Earth is good for Metal, but Metal exhausts Earth
Metal is good for Water, but Water exhausts Metal.

To fine tune the analysis, here is an example of the elements being used constructively:

To energize the wood element of the southeast, we can introduce a water feature (eg a fountain or bird bath). This brings additional helpful energy to the southeast. But to energize the water element of the north, we should not introduce a wood feature (eg a plant) as this merely draws from the water of the north, thereby exhausting it. The result is a weakening of the intrinsic energy of the north, even though the two elements of wood and water are not in disharmony.

It is far better to energize the water of the north with the introduction of a metal container, which symbolically holds water. This is because metal produces water while wood exhausts water.

The destructive cycle of the elements

This is the opposite of the productive cycle. The cycle demonstrates how the severe hostility of certain element combinations can lead to destruction. They are exactly the combination of elements that we should continually endeavour to avoid.

The destructive cycle illustrates how one element can be hostile to another. For practical purposes therefore, it suggests that placing a metal feature in a wood corner would be disastrous since metal destroys wood. Consider, however, the effect of small metal on big wood; here, the deadliness of the metal against wood is balanced by the size of the wood element. In the process, it transforms the relation between metal and wood into an enhancing one because small metal (in the form of tools) can enhance the value of wood (eg when it becomes furniture).

In the same way, take the case of fire and metal. Fire is said to destroy metal, and yet without the heat of fire, how can ornaments and jewellery be produced?

Or the case of fire and water. Water is said to put out fire and so is bad for fire, so the two elements should be kept far apart. But when you consider that fire turns water into steam, which represents power, in certain circumstances, the relationship of fire and water can be an auspicious one.

Balancing yin and yang

The influence of yin and yang cosmology in the practice of feng shui is a universal reflection of the way the Chinese view the Earth's energies. Ideally, everyone and everything should be in a state of balance. Then things occur smoothly. When the energies are out of sync, problems start and troubles occur. Yin and yang are viewed as primordial forces that possess completely opposing attributes. Yet despite these, or perhaps because of it, one gives existence to the other. Without yin there is simply no yang, and vice versa.

The attributes of yin and yang

YIN is dark, stillness, lifelessness, and death.
YIN is the moon, the night time hours, the negative
YIN is the cold, it is the valley, and stagnant water
YIN is the female, passive, weak, soft and yielding.

YANG is light, brightness, sunlight, the sun
YANG is activity, sounds, fire, strength, determination
YANG is movement, life, raised landforms, mountains, the dragon
YANG is the male, dominant, hard, warm, heat.

Yin and yang continually interact, creating change. Thus summer, which is yang, gives way to winter, which is yin, which then becomes summer again. Night becomes day. The moon gives way to the sun. Darkness becomes light … and so forth. Applying yin and yang to the environment to understand the forces that affect feng shui requires a perfect understanding of the nature and essence of yin and yang energy. Neither is good nor bad. One must be seen in relation to the other. Like the theory of elements, yin/yang forces must be viewed, one in terms of the other.

In the feng shui of houses for the living (as opposed to houses for the dead), yang energy should dominate, though never to the extent that it completely overshadows yin energy. This is especially true of rooms occupied by growing children since they need healthy doses of yang energy. In rooms where sick people are convalescing, the strong presence of yang energy helps the body to heal.

Yang energy is vibrant and alive with life. It glows and shines, bringing good fortune. But the minute yang overpowers yin completely, yang itself ceases to exist. Rooms and houses should allow yang to dominate but not to completely deplete yin energy, especially in the bedrooms, which are places of rest and relaxation that benefit from dominant yin energies. Yet, here again, the yin must not be so strong as to totally annihilate yang energy.

The key to yin and yang balance therefore is to have the right mix, based on what kind of room is being assessed. The correct balance of yin and yang depends almost entirely on the use of the room, and on what the building is being used for.

Yin and yang energy in the office

Commercial buildings and shopping places should be made very yang with lots of bright colours, activity, and noise, with an air of positive energy. In such places, the yang energy brings good business luck. The Chinese always decorate their commercial shops and restaurants with healthy doses of yang energies by using plenty of red. They also keep the front part of their shops well lit, which is also very yang.

Offices benefit from plenty of yang energy so ensure that interior decorators don't get too carried away and make the office so yin that business suffers. This happens when there is an excess of quiet, of grey steel cabinets, of dark coloured walls and dark silent corners. Offices like these are so quiet and so yin they symbolize death. There are many examples of this sort of office. Long corridors with rooms opening off them resembling cells compound the excessive yin with shar chi (see pages 52-3) energy as well. The feng shui of such an office is not good

Yang offices are always bright and airy; the energies are never stale or stagnant. Such offices are also clean and made to come alive with healthy yang plants. When there is music playing, yang energies get a further boost and feng shui is improved still further. Boardrooms benefit from a window view, which also brings in the light. Planters add to the feeling of life and activity. These are yang features, adding to the feng shui of the office.

Yin and yang energy in the home

Residential homes do not require the same amounts of yang energy as that required in a working environment. Nevertheless yang should still dominate. Too much yin energy cause illness, loss and even death. If the home is too quiet, especially during the day when everyone is out at work or are at school, yin energy will accumulate. In such situations, keeping pets

Develop sensitivity to killing energies

Much of feng shui effectiveness in the office comes from a sensitivity to the energies that surround your workspace. I remember years ago when we corrected the feng shui of the dealing room of our bank's treasury department, I observed the feng shui master as he identified one poison arrow after another in the small, cramped and cluttered space. Dealing rooms are always untidy. Often they are dirty and stale as well – filled with the air of left-over cigarettes – and these cause the energies of the space to become drenched with negative energies that are much too yin.

We cleaned up our dealing room, gave it a coat of fresh paint, re-arranged the furniture to make sure none of the dealers were sitting under exposed ceiling beams and sharp edges of corners. From then on, our dealing room regularly reported stable, and at times, even quite outstanding performance in the money and foreign exchange markets. It was experiences such as these, which added to my conviction that feng shui was a very useful management tool.

Yang energy represents growth, life and activity, while yin energy symbolizes death, darkness and an absence of activity. In business, yang energy is almost vital for survival. This is the reason why red is considered to be such an auspicious colour – because red symbolizes precious yang energy. So, tune in to the quality of your workspace. If the air is musty and damp from years of air conditioning, then open the windows and let the sunshine in. Replace dirty old curtains that have never been washed, or are so faded as to be crying out for change. All of these situations create an excess of yin energy. Often, simply letting the light in by opening windows will clear the air.

But feng shui is also about balance. Yang energies must not become so excessive as to become harmful. Thus, when your office gets directly exposed to the noonday and afternoon sun, the glare and the heat of too much sunshine causes the air to become charged with killing energy. Yin has become non-existent, as a result of which imbalance has been created. In situations like this there are two methods of getting things right. Either use curtains or heavy blinds to shut out the sun in the afternoons, or hang a whole series of faceted crystal balls to break the sun's rays into healthy and balancing rainbows. The full spectrum of colours restores the balance of yin and yang. More, the rainbow lights attract precious sheng chi, or the growth energy, and this is especially good for business feng shui.

helps. The presence of life, in the form of cats or dogs, plants, goldfish or bubbling water, all cause yang energy to flow ensuring that the yin/yang balance stays right. Alternatively, keep a moving lamp turned on at home while you are at work so that yin energies do not begin to accumulate.

An excess of yang energy also cause imbalance. When the hot bright afternoon sun shines relentlessly into the home, this brings in too much yang. Close off some of the bright sunlight with shades. When a house is too noisy with too many people; where the colours are too overpowering, and when music blares out from the radio, excessive yang energy is created – causing hot tempers, a great deal of shouting, and other, similar, manifestations of excessive energy. Counter the excess yang with darker colours. Dim the lights, and keep curtains closed.

The dragon's cosmic breath

Beneficial, meandering chi.

The dragon's breath is the central theme of Chinese feng shui. This is a symbolic reference to the beneficial energy that is said to swirl around the environment. Described as the magical life force, chi pervades every place in the Universe and the aim of feng shui is to select natural environments that have an abundance of chi, or to create homes and buildings that successfully attract an abundance of chi.

To do the former successfully requires experience in assessing the natural landforms and topography of the land, and to successfully create or attract chi requires an understanding of its characteristics.

Beneficial versus harmful chi

Sheng chi

To start with, it is necessary to appreciate that beneficial chi, known in Chinese as sheng chi, always meanders slowly. It never moves fast. It never moves in a straight line. In places where there is a good balance of yin and yang energy, it tends to settle and accumulate. Chi also requires the air to be fresh and clean. When the atmosphere gets overly damp, wet, dry or hot, chi becomes stale. And when the place is dirty, chi also turns foul.

Beneficial chi brings good fortune and is described as vibrant, energetic and full of vigour. It is different from the wind, but it travels with the wind. It exists in the air, under the ground, in water and in the human body. Human chi is viewed as a life force which gives focused strength to martial arts' exponents and special skills to artists and artisans. Chinese healing methods and health foods use chi analysis to diagnose for blockages in the flow of chi within the human body.

In feng shui, the chi which flows around a home should not get blocked. When plumbing does not work, it is advisable to get it fixed as soon as possible. When drains get blocked, the luck of the family suffers. At the same time, the design of doors and windows that lead the flow of chi from room to room within a home should always make it meander, and never allow it to travel in a straight line.

When chi gathers speed, it becomes harmful. For this reason, a major taboo of feng shui is the three doors in a straight-line configuration (see page 95). A variation of this is the deadly mirror that directly reflects the main door. This is said to cause chi to enter the home and fly straight out again. So while mirrors can be a panacea for many feng shui ills, they must be used very carefully, and it is especially vital to remember that mirrors should never reflect the main door (see page 94). Otherwise the patriarch will succumb to illness and disease.

Chi is said to stop and settle each time it encounters water, which is why water features are said to be auspicious. In feng shui, water always represents money and the presence of water near a home tends to bring good luck to the front door. But water must be orientated correctly for its full benefits to be reaped.

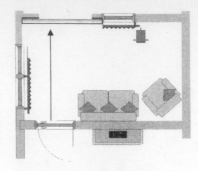

Above: Mirrors should be positioned carefully in the home. Never hang a mirror directly behind the front door as it causes chi to enter the home and then fly straight out again.

Left: A water feature in the home brings good luck the to the front door.

Shar chi

Feng shui also addresses the presence of hostile energies within the living environments. These energies, referred to as the killing breath or shar chi, cause intense bad luck. Sometimes it causes death to those who reside in buildings or rooms which lie in its path, or get hit by this killing breath. In feng shui, this hostile breath is said to be caused by structures, natural and man-made, that are deemed to be sending secret poison arrows in a straight line outwards.

Feng shui shows you how to avoid, defuse and deflect these hostile energies. A great deal of misfortune, ranging from frequent illnesses to loss of jobs and incomes, downturns in your fortunes, quarrels, breakups and relationship problems, are caused by there being something wrong in the feng shui of the home. More often than not this is due to the presence of hostile energies that have been inadvertently created by poison arrows. When these arrows hit directly at your main door, the bad luck created is extremely serious, especially when the structure that represents the poison arrow is heavy, massive, very sharp and pointed, and thus very hostile. Examples of this are the edge of a big building, or a straight road, or simply the triangular roof line of a neighbour's house and it then becomes necessary to protect your home against

The edge of this building represents a deadly poison arrow. Anything sharp, pointed or straight has the potential of becoming a poison arrow.

such a poison arrow. Feng shui is all about identifying these arrows in the environment around you and then deflecting them.

Living with the flow of chi

The physical features of the environment affect the intrinsic nature of chi. Whether it is auspicious or not depends on how surrounding hills and mountains encourage it to settle or cause it to dissipate. Man-made structures also affect the flow of chi. When buildings, roads and highways blend harmoniously with the natural surroundings, the flow of chi is enhanced and its beneficial qualities magnified. In the vicinity of hostile sharp or angular structures, however, chi gets transformed into harmful energy.

Living by roads

Try to avoid living at the end of a road. Here chi is said to stagnate. If your luck changes for the worse, such a configuration magnifies your bad luck situation as it symbolizes no way out of your problems. When you are going through a good period, living in a dead end will not create problems. But when you are going through a tough time, it compounds the bad luck

Another positive suggestion is that you should try to avoid living in a house or building that directly faces an oncoming straight road. This is the classical T-junction which is regarded as so harmful the bad chi which enters your home is said to be a killer. The effect is lethal.

If you live near winding roads or when there is a curved road in front of your house, it is better to be on the inside of the curve than on the

Living by roads

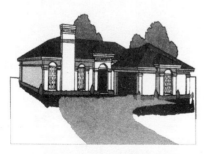

Above: Bad feng shui is caused by living at a dead end.

Right: The deadly chi of a straight road can be blocked off with a hedge, a wall, or some trees.

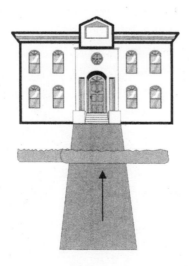

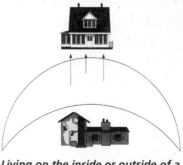

Living on the inside or outside of a curve in a road can effect the feng shui of your home. The house on the inside of this curved road enjoys the benevolent breath! The house on the outside of the curve has inausicious feng shui.

outside. When your house is located outside the curve, the road becomes a knife that symbolically cuts into your house (see illustration on the previous page). The chi at this side of the road is malevolent, while the chi on the other side is benevolent. So always make sure the road embraces your house. In the illustration on the previous page, the house that is hugged by the road has much better feng shui than the house opposite.

The level of a house

Straight roads and T-junctions do not hurt you if your house sits on elevated land. The deadly chi cannot reach homes that are located higher than the road. On the other hand, if your house sits on land that is lower than the road, you should symbolically raise the chi of your house with lights. Or better yet, build another level to your house so that your roof level becomes higher than the road. Even better, do both!

The chi that stays below road level is never auspicious. It is for this reason that overseas Chinese who emigrate to live in Western countries prefer to avoid basement flats. They do not relish the thought of living in basement flats unless there is a level garden to compensate for the below road level. Even then, sleeping below road level causes residents to suffer from bad fortune chi.

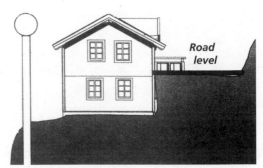

If your house is lower than surrounding land, erect a light behind the house to enhance the chi.

Nearby constructions

It is also not a good idea to live in a one-level house that is sandwiched between two multi-level and large imposing houses. These houses are said to block the flow of benevolent chi towards your house, thereby adversely affecting your feng shui. The same rule applies to commercial buildings in the city. To correct the problem, put a light on the ground next to your home so that its bulb faces upwards.

Do not live too near anything that is higher, larger or taller than your house if it faces your front door. This can be a high wall, the edge of a large building, or simply elevated land. All these are examples of structures which will

A house sandwiched between two taller ones can suffer from bad feng shui because of shar chi being aimed at the smaller house.

completely block any beneficial chi from entering your home. If you are presently living in such a house, chances are your luck has not been good. The nearer the offending structure, the more severe is the bad luck, which can come in the form of illness, loss of income and jobs, and nothing going right at home or at work.

Traffic flows

Understanding the way in which chi moves offers valuable clues to the way roads affect the feng shui of your home. Generally, it is not a good idea to live too close to roads and highways where the traffic moves exceedingly fast. Like the traffic, chi also moves much too fast, bringing harmful misfortune. It is, however, considered good luck to be located near heavy traffic roads if the traffic moves slowly, but does not get stuck, as in a traffic jam.

If you live in a residential area, traffic rarely moves fast enough to be harmful unless there is a flyover or an overpass nearby. These elevated roadways can cause horrible feng shui for those affected by them. If you live too close to such a flyover – less than one third of a mile – my suggestion is that you should put some really tall trees between your house and the highway. Or, if you have the option to do so, simply move out!

Deflecting the killing breath

It is not possible to itemize everything that can potentially represent a poison arrow. It is also not necessary to develop paranoia about this aspect of feng shui practice to the extent that you start seeing poison arrows where none exist. Remember that for any structure in the environment to hurt you it should have the following characteristics. If you can answer yes to all of these questions, then and only then is the structure or object hurting your home. Otherwise you should relax.

1 Is the structure sharp, pointed or straight?

2 Is it directly facing your main door, in a straight line?

3 Is it larger and taller than your house?

4 Does it resemble a hostile shape such as anything that can hurt, like the shape of a fierce animal like a tiger, or in the shape of a knife, gun or bow and arrow? Anything that suggests hostility is bad.

5 Does it seem poised, about to collapse onto your house?

If facing sharp edges

The most serious of poison arrows are those caused by man-made constructions – and these range from the massive high-rise buildings that are found in cities to factories, supermarkets and other shopping malls that are now commonplace

Below: Note the triangle of this roof line. It becomes a lethal poison arrow if it directly faces your main door.

Above and below: The sharp edges of buildings emit a great deal of killing breath. Make sure your door does not face such an edge. In the city, the four corners of office towers give off shar chi, while in the suburbs, the edges of supermarket malls could be hurting you.

A clump of trees is an excellent feng shui cure.

in the suburbs. These buildings are not harmful per se. They only become dangerous to you if your house and its main door directly face the sharp edges caused by their corners. In feng shui terms few things are as dangerous as the sharp edge of a big building. In Taiwan, many of the buildings in downtown Taipei have their edges rounded out to soften the edges of their buildings. This results in less harm being done to their neighbours, so reducing the chances of retaliation with a Pa Kua mirror!

Probably as harmful as a sharp edge is the triangular roof line of a huge building or a neighbour's house. I have seen some extremely fierce looking roof lines that emit huge doses of bad luck to anyone unfortunate enough to be facing them. These are sharply angled with the apex pointing directly at your front door.

The best way of countering the examples of poison arrows illustrated opposite is to create a barrier of some kind that effectively shields your house from their bad energy. The best barrier is tall, big trees as the rustling

The bright hall effect

One of the most auspicious feng shui features anyone can have is to have their main door face a park, a football field, or any kind of empty land. This creates what feng shui masters refer to as the bright hall effect and it is truly extremely auspicious. If your home faces just such a bright hall, your luck will be very good indeed.

However, if there is a statue like the one shown here, and if the statue is directly facing your front door, then the statue will have become a deadly poison arrow that threatens the good fortune created by the bright hall. It is then necessary to block out the view of the statue, or to re-orientate your door, even at the cost of giving up your most auspicious bright hall! This example should make it clear how feng shui can and should be practised.

This lucky house faces a bright hall which brings abundant good fortune. If the door directly faces an obstacle like a statue, however, the good luck is counterbalanced.

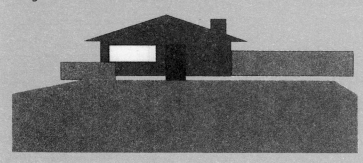

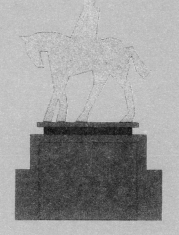

leaves create a curtain of energy that transforms and softens the killing shar chi into something less harmful. If the poison arrow is being caused by the roof line of your neighbour's very small house, then hanging a wind chime should do the job successfully.

If facing large or elevated structures

This is like confronting something that will overwhelm you. The most common example is when you are directly facing a brick wall, the side of a hill, a large building, or – worst of all – a huge mountain. To combat this situation, try to close up the door that directly confronts the big building or wall. Use another door, enabling you

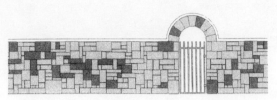

Don't let your main door open to a brick wall too close by.

to effectively change the orientation of your home so that the threatening building, wall or hill is turned into back support. In short, get it behind you!

If you cannot reposition your door, install a bright light just outside it to strengthen the yang energy. Keep the lights turned on for the best part of the early evening and night. It also helps if you paint your door a bright red since this also creates precious yang energy which effectively counters the negative energy coming from across the road. Alternatively, hang a wind chime to transform the stifled energy so it becomes less negative.

When the elevated structure that faces your home is further away, the inauspicious effect is not so pronounced, especially if there are trees between your home and the offending structure. Trees are excellent for countering harmful chi energy. Nevertheless, structures like transmission towers, large chimneys of factories or telecommunication towers, do send out massive doses of shar chi - the killing breath - and these usually cause illness to those affected. Electricity transmission towers are especially harmful, and try to avoid living too near to one.

Facing a tower like this is bad luck. Trees are great for countering harmful chi energy; grow them between your home and position a large structure, if you have one, in front of you.

A bridge, too, can be harmful.

Other potentially harmful structures, which could cause feng shui problems for you are bridges, power stations and other massive concrete and steel edifices. Be extremely wary of these man-made constructions. They can be very threatening if they directly face your home. Try to ensure they are behind you and always plant some trees to create a barrier of leaves between them and your home.

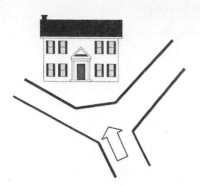

Left: Y-junctions can be as deadly as T-junctions.

Left: The dangerous position of living at the end of a T-junction.

If facing harmful junctions

These are really bad news, especially when the junction results in a straight road coming straight at your front door. In feng shui this situation is said to be akin to night tigers attacking your home. The front lights of oncoming cars do indeed resemble the fierce energies of the tigers in the night. Look at the two classical harmful junctions illustrated above. See how, in each case, the buildings, and especially their respective front doors, are positioned directly in the path of harmful energy coming from the road.

If you are living with such a configuration, and if your main door (or your entrance gate) is being hit by such poisonous shar chi, I strongly suggest that you use a corrective measure. Build a barrier of some kind if you can afford to, by planting a hedge or a clump of trees, or by building a low wall.

If places are too yin

Places that are considered to have an excessive amount of yin energy are places that are associated with death. It is considered most inauspicious to live near cemeteries, hospitals, abattoirs, funeral homes, and police stations, for example. Living in the vicinity of such places causes your home to be shrouded with too much yin energy resulting in you and your family succumbing to the debilitating effects of excessive yin energy so you feel listless, de-motivated and negative.

Five effective cures

Here are five extremely effective cures against a harmful junction that is hurting your home. These methods are based on the compass formulas.

1 Hang a curved knife if the road is coming from the east or southeast.
2 Place a large boulder between your door and the road if the road is coming from the north.
3 Place a bright spotlight and shine outwards from above your door if the road is coming from the west or northwest.
4 Place an urn of water in front of your house if the offending road is coming from the south.
5 Plant a clump of trees in front of the house if the offending road comes at you from the southwest or northeast.

Right: If your house directly faces a cemetery, hospital, police station or a funeral parlour, an effective counter is to re-paint your door yellow, red, white or orange.

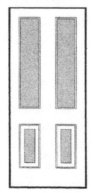

The way to combat such a situation is to balance the excessive yin energy with large doses of yang energy. This means painting your front door in a bright yang colour (red, yellow, orange or white), keeping your radio turned on through the day to create the yang of sound and music, and install plenty of bright lights. You do not need to move away just because you live near a cemetery, for example. Just block off the view of the cemetery and then counter the negative energies with yang energy.

Another very effective way of accumulating precious yang energy is to have lots of plants in your garden. Anything that symbolizes growth and activity is yang: keeping yappy little dogs is always a great idea! There is nothing to beat pets to simulate vital yang energy.

If you are directly facing a hospital, the best way of countering the negative energy is to grow a clump of trees to block off the view and to install a tall spotlight that shines upwards. This serve to raise the energy around your home, and it effectively counters any negative energy that may be directed at your house, or surrounding the vicinity of your home.

If you face an abattoir or funeral parlour, the death energy is very strong. The most effective way of countering this negative energy is to use the yang colour red which is an extremely powerful colour.

If places emit a foul breath

The nature of good feng shui always presumes a healthy, vibrant and clean environment, where everything is in working order. Thus my first piece of advice to friends who ask me how they can have good feng shui is to make sure their homes are well maintained. It sounds innocuous, but peeling paint and defective plumbing and lighting suggest stagnant and stale energies, and these are the bane of feng shui.

Other things that create foul breath around the home are stagnant drains and blocked sewage pipes. You must always make sure that water in, around or near your house never gets blocked, and is not allowed to become stagnant. Dirty and polluted drains also cause foul breath, and sometimes they even cause there to be a stench. These are harmful to the energies around your home and should be got rid of. Make it a habit to check these matters at least once a month. The practice of feng shui is not a

The colour red
The colour red has always been deemed to be an auspicious colour to the Chinese. It is a colour that is used to symbolize all the happy occasions of mankind and so is widely used during the important days like the New Year, and wedding and birth celebrations. On the first day of the lunar New Year, Chinese wear red to ensure they are wrapped in yang energy on this vitally important day. Brides also always wear red for this same reason, and births are celebrated with hard boiled eggs dyed a deep dark red for continued fertility luck.

one time thing. To enjoy good feng shui all year round it is always necessary to check on drains, trees and plants, as well as other changes taking place in the environment.

The worst form of foul breath is for your main door to be directly facing a rubbish heap, or a garbage can. I have repeatedly told a neighbour to remove the horrible rubbish bin she places directly in front of her main door. I remind her each time she asks me to help her do her feng shui. Yet she always forgets to carry out my advice. I was not surprised when told that her husband's business went bust, and that she had succumbed to an illness. This is a good time for me to reiterate that feng shui is not something terribly elaborate or mysterious. A simple thing like putting the garbage out of sight of the main door, for instance, is feng shui.

Imagine this heap of rubbish and garbage in front of your main door. Can it bring you anything but bad feng shui?

Feng shui tools for deterring shar chi

In this section, I will go into detail on how you can use ordinary objects to correct common feng shui problems. In feng shui, what is blocked from view is deemed to have been effectively deflected to some extent unless the object sending that bad energy is very large and therefore very fierce. Under ordinary circumstances, screens, plants, furniture and other ordinary articles commonly available can be orchestrated to become excellent feng shui tools. It is not necessary to purchase special Pa Kua mirrors, wind chimes, or elaborate Chinese compasses to counter the killing breath of bad energy. Although these traditional objects of protection are wonderful if you can obtain them, they are not the only tools that can be used.

Pa Kua mirrors

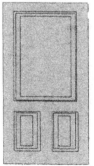

In recent years, awareness and appreciation of the wonderful octagonal Pa Kua shape has grown in leaps and bounds but remember that you have to use the yin Pa Kua where the trigrams are in the Early Heaven Arrangement (see page 22). You can buy such a Pa Kua from any local Chinatown store, but do be very careful. The protective Pa Kua, for instance, has become well known as an extremely powerful feng shui tool, and indeed it is. Hung outside the office and above an entrance door it deflects a multitude of bad energy. It is especially useful when used to counter the killing breath of trees, straight roads, bad junctions and harmful roof lines.

The Pa Kua should, however, be used with care. It is a very powerful symbol, and it works by sending out powerful negative energy of its own to counter bad energy coming at your doorway. Its potency is believed to

A Pa Kua mirror hung above a main door on the outside to deter the shar chi of an offensive road junction. It should never be hung inside.

derive not just from its shape but also from the mirror in its centre, and from the placement of the trigrams around it.

It is absolutely vital that you should never place this Pa Kua inside your office or your house. If you need to counter problems with your interior feng shui, use one or more of the other tools suggested below, but do not use the Pa Kua. If you do, everyone at home or in the office will start fighting with each other. Relationships and productivity will suffer and where before your problems were small ones, now they will become big. In fact, I actively discourage the use of the Pa Kua because in deflecting feng shui problems, it inadvertently hurts others. It would be far better to use other, less harmful, feng shui cures.

Equally, mirrors in the bedroom are not a good idea. Whether they are on walls or on the ceiling, mirrors should be avoided unless they are put there for the specific purpose of, say, correcting a missing corner (see page 36). In fact, when using mirrors, whatever the reason, it is a good idea to take proper precautions and ensure that in solving one problem you are not inadvertently creating another.

Mirrors in the living room could be inadvertently reflecting the main door which would be inauspicious for this room as it is associated with wealth. As for mirror tiles, these are bad news anywhere in the house since they create havoc with reflections. Avoid them like the plague as they 'cut' into people through distorted reflections, thereby creating negative energy.

Above: A healthy plant bring healthy energy to a room.

Below: A dead plant, however, does not.

Plants

These are extremely wonderful feng shui cures and they make excellent stimulants. As a corrective device, there are some guidelines to follow.

Be clever in your choice of plants. In an office environment, choose plants that are hardy. It is likely that in the office, plants will suffer from lack of care, lack of sunlight and lack of the great outdoors. So do not expect them to thrive. It might be better to have them replaced regularly, probably each month. Use a garden supplier who can do this. Sick plants are bad feng shui.

Real plants are a better idea than fake plants. Artificial plants can be used as feng shui tools, but real plants emit better quantities of yang energy. However, if you prefer to use professionally made silk plants in the interest of easier maintenance, they are acceptable. I have used silk maples and ficus trees for years with great success. If you prefer silk, select those plants that have good balanced foliage

Left: It is preferable to use real plants rather than fake; and replace them as soon as they start to look tired and jaded.

Place a healthy creeper plant directly against the sharp edge of a square pillar, a protruding corner, or an edge formed by two walls. This is an effective way of deflecting the killing breath created by the sharp edge.

A cactus plant placed outside the office door effectively counters the bad chi of staircases, elevators and lifts that directly face the door.

like the one illustrated here. Please note that even fake plants have to be replenished each year because when the leaves look faded, like the real thing, they too, lose their yang energy. Likewise, dried flowers which are obviously dead give off too much yin energy so do not keep them in your home or office.

Never place plants that have thorns or whose leaves look like needles inside the office. In this respect, I discourage the display of prickled cactus plants. Even when placed at windowsills as ornaments, these thorny beauties emit tiny slivers of killing breath that hurt you without you realiz-ing. Cactus plants, however, can be used as a feng shui device when placed just outside the main door of the office. A pair of cactus plants, for example, can effectively deflect the ill effects of a main door that faces staircases, elevators, and lift doors. If they are being used in this manner, the plants should be fairly large in size. Remember, too, that they must be placed outside the office, not inside.

Tie red ribbons or string onto a pair of hollow bamboo stems and hang them as shown to counter the heavy killing breath of exposed overhead beams.

Bamboo stems

Bamboo stems are another effective and easily available feng shui aid and I refer to them very frequently in this book. The effect of bamboo stems is similar to that created by the use of wind chimes and flutes. The only thing missing from the use of bamboo stems is the tinkling sound or the symbolic music suggested by the use of flutes. It is for this reason that I recommend tying a red string or a red ribbon to the bamboo. This symbolically activates the channelling properties of the bamboo stem, thereby encouraging hostile chi to flow through the stem and emerge, slowed down and transformed into good energy. The bamboo is regarded as a potent symbol of longevity and harmony, and feng shui texts often accord it an important place in the spectrum of the practice.

Important things to remember about wind chimes

1 The rods that make up the wind chime should be hollow and open at both ends. Solid wind chimes have no feng shui effect because wind chimes work via the chanelling method which attracts chi through the hollows of the rods, in the process changing the bad energy into good energy.

2 Wind chimes can be made of wood, metal (copper, aluminium, steel or even silver), and porcelain. Select the appropriate material for the corner where you need to hang your wind chime as follows:

If your wind chime is being used as a protective measure to overcome a bad corner or an overhanging beam:

* hang a metal wind chime in the east or southeast.
* hang a wood wind chime in the northeast or southwest
* hang a ceramic wind chime in the north.

If the wind chime is not being used as a corrective tool, the type of wind chime used should be different:

* hang a wood wind chime in the east and southeast
* hang a ceramic wind chime in the north-east and southwest
* hang a metal wind chime in the west and the northwest.

3 Take note of the number of rods the wind chime has. Wind chimes that are used for the purpose of overcoming shar chi should always have five rods. Wind chimes that are used for enhancing different corners should be designed as follows:

for the southwest: 2 rods
for the east: 3 rods
for the southeast: 4 rods
for the northwest: 6 rods
for the west: 7 rods
for the northeast: 8 rods
for the south: 9 rods.

Wind chimes

Wind chimes come in a variety of styles. The growing popularity of feng shui in recent years has stimulated a great deal of creativity among wind chime manufacturers, so these wonderful tinkling implements are now quite easily available at mind, body and spirit exhibitions and there are a great variety of simple wind chimes available from Chinese supermarkets and curio stores in the Chinatowns of the world.

Wind chimes are not mobiles. It is not necessary to have fish and other objects hung with the rods. Indeed, these objects can be harmful if they are sharp or pointed. If you are buying wind chimes, choose the traditional styles. Chinese wind chimes that come with pagodas and the double happiness signs are excellent. They are also cheap and small. Nevertheless, they are no less potent, and they do the job very efficiently. Hang the wind chime high up a room to encourage chi to flow upwards and through the rods, thereby benefiting the whole house.

Screens and dividers

These may not be very suitable in the general office, but they make the most wonderful corrective tool for office rooms that are badly shaped. In an L-shaped room, for example, the screen or room divider is excellent for creating two regular shaped sections to the whole room. When using screens, there are two useful tips to keep in mind.

1 Choose screens that are decorated with auspicious, decorative objects. All Oriental screens – Chinese or Japanese – usually come with very auspicious paintings of cranes, lotuses, legends, deities or good fortune trees, fruits and flowers. It is an excellent idea to choose any of these screens for your office room since they would give you the added benefit of being symbolically auspicious as well. If you prefer something more modern, just make certain you do not choose screens that are decorated with angular designs. Some of the art deco styles can be quite harmful; art nouveau designs with curving lines represent much better feng shui.

2 When you display screens and use them as room dividers, do not stand them in a zigzag fashion, even though this was how they were envisaged to be. Instead, hang them suspended from the ceiling in a straight panel, or have them firmly anchored to the floor, also in a straight line. If they are displayed in zigzag fashion, they create too many edges that emit shar chi into the room, thus becoming poison arrows.

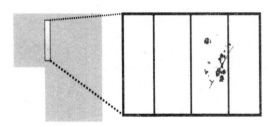

Use a screen with an auspicious design as a room divider to regularize an L-shaped office room. Make sure you place the screen standing upright and straight rather than in a wavy zigzag fashion. Screens that are placed in a zigzag fashion create poison arrows in the room.

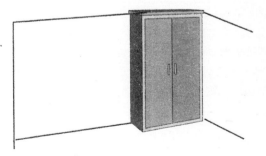

Have furniture that fits neatly into corners for good feng shui.

Using symbols and numbers

Symbolism is an essential part of feng shui. In the language of the ancients, a great deal was communicated through and hidden in symbols. Feng shui incorporates vital appreciation of auspicious signs and representations and these range from flowers, fruits and trees to birds and animals. An entire encyclopedia can be written to adequately cover all the meanings of all the symbols.

The Chinese also have a whole pantheon of deities that are paragons of the virtues and aspirations symbolizing the good life. There are Gods of Wealth and Longevity, and there are deities that protect and defend. From the animal world come the deer and the crane, which symbolize longevity; the elephant who denotes strength and good fortune; the tiger and the lion dogs, who protect and guard.

There are celestial animals that are believed to bring extreme good fortune, creatures whose existence is mythical and legendary. In feng shui, dragon and phoenix symbolism are deemed to be present when there are elevated land forms in the nearby environment. These, together with the tiger and the turtle, are always associated with surrounding hills and mountains. Thus three peaks seen within view of the home is deemed exceptionally fortunate for the eldest son of the family. Who knows if dragons and phoenixes really exist. As far as the Chinese are concerned, whether or not they do are not matters of vital importance. What is significant is that their symbolic presence, manifested in hills and mountains, will bring auspicious good fortune.

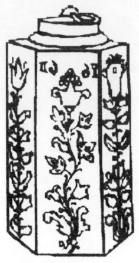

The symbolic presence of flowers and animals are peaceful additions to any home.

The symbolic presence of auspicious objects – flowers or animals – can be in the form of their images, either painted and hung on the wall, or fashioned into works of ceramic art. It is for this reason that almost all works of art coming out of China depict either good fortune flowers, animals or deities, or they show the legends that demonstrate some aspect of good fortune. In particular, legends of the Eight Immortals are favourite subjects since immortality and long life are two favourite all-time aspirations of the Chinese.

In terms of symbolism, the two most popular aspirations found in a Chinese home are wealth and longevity. So the three Star Gods, Fuk Luk

Sau (the Gods of wealth, health and longevity) are ever present. These three Gods (seldom worshipped but always displayed) are believed to bring a great deal of excellent good fortune that includes both prosperity and long life. They can be bought from any supermarket but please note that they are symbolic entities; not Gods or Deities to be worshipped.

The God of Longevity − Sau − is almost always depicted with the other two symbols of longevity − the deer and the peach. Sometimes the pine tree, another symbol of longevity, is included if the tableau is shown in a Chinese scroll painting.

Numbers and their meanings

The symbolism of numbers brings additional dimensions to the practice of feng shui. The Chinese are especially careful when it comes to the important numbers that rule their business and professional life. They always go to great lengths so that their telephone and fax numbers end with either of the lucky numbers 8 or 9.

◆ The number 8 is considered extremely auspicious. To the Cantonese, this is due to the phonetic sound of the number which sounds like growth in riches. But even according to the Lo Shu numerology of feng shui, 8 is a prosperous number that refers to continued prosperity into the future.

◆ The number 9 is another lucky number, and some say this is an even better number than 8 since 9 symbolizes the fullness of heaven and earth. (It is the only number which added any number of times still result in 9, eg 9 times 3 is 27, and 2 plus 7 gives 9. Do this with any number of times you multiply 9 with …) It is thus a number that cannot be corrupted.

◆ The Chinese also regard the number 7 as being very lucky because, according to the Chinese calendar, we are presently going through the

The number 9

This number represents continued prosperity far into the future. In Hong Kong, my friend Dickson Poon once told me that the best gift his late father gave him was the car registration number 9999, which he fixed to his Rolls Royce. In those days, Dickson was only a 15-shop retailer. Today, this erstwhile entrepreneur has built a worldwide retailing giant that owns Harvey Nichols of London, ST Dupont of Paris and Barneys of the USA.

Dickson's other cars carry the registration numbers 928 which is also considered an extremely favourable number. This is because it means easy to grow and expand with prosperity.

period of 7. This period will last until the year 2003 when the number changes to 8. After the year 2003, the number 8 will then be doubly auspicious.

◆ Combinations of the numbers 7, 8, and 9 in any configuration are highly prized. Chinese retailers love pricing their goods to end with 8, as in $388 or $28.88 or $3,988. They believe this brings luck to both buyer and seller.

◆ Meanwhile, the number 4 is regarded as being inauspicious. Anything that ends in this number spells death, loss and problems. Thus, level 14 in a multi-storey building carries bad luck connotations that are even more severe than the western 13 (which, incidentally, is regarded as auspicious to the Chinese).

◆ House addresses that have the dreaded 4 usually cannot get sold, while apartments on level 4 are hugely unpopular. Having said this, it is interesting to note that 44 and 48 are regarded as being extremely auspicious. This is because the double 4 adds up to the wonderful 8 and the 48 means a whole lot of that auspicious number 8! (Yes, I know ... it is not easy to follow Chinese logic!)

Formula feng shui

The Lo Shu numbers form the basis for calculating auspicious and inauspicious dates contained in the *Tong Shu*, or *Chinese Almanac*, a reference book of good and bad days of the year which is an annual bestseller in Hong Kong and Taiwan. It is used in these countries and elsewhere for doing a multitude of activities, from launching new ventures to signing agreements, to moving house and travel *et al*. Most Chinese business people would seldom make any important decisions or launch any major undertaking without consulting the *Tong Shu*.

The almanac also contains valuable calculations of flying star feng shui, an advanced formula that is extremely popular with the practitioners in Hong Kong. Flying star feng shui is an excellent technique used for pinpointing the exact lucky and unlucky corners of any house or building for each day, week, and month of the year. It is said that using this method, the experts can forecast when serious illness will strike occupants who have their bedrooms in certain corners; or when a house will get burgled based on the location of the front door. Or when a serious calamity will hit a family, once again based on the location of the main door coming into conflict with really bad combinations of flying stars.

Flying star feng shui

This branch of feng shui is based on the arrangement of the numbers of the Lo Shu square. It is an advanced branch of feng shui, and the computations are complex. An easy way of using flying stars, however, is to have the computations made out for future years by a feng shui master, and then to apply the findings to your own home. Simplified representations of these computations are given overleaf.

Flying star feng shui is a popular method of feng shui which addresses the time aspects of feng shui. It complements the space dimension of the feng shui concepts described so far, and it offers a method for calculating the luck of every corner of every room in any given year, month or twenty year period. In addition, the technique of flying star feng shui also offers a specific method of drawing out the natal chart of every building, home or apartment.

A feng shui master versed in this method can cast a natal chart for any house or building, and merely by studying the numbers and combination of numbers he can describe the luck of all the corners of the home. He is thus able to describe unfortunate consequences befalling residents of certain unlucky rooms, and also offer predictive warnings against sleeping or working in certain unlucky rooms. It is the numbers, and combination of numbers, which tell the feng shui master what kind of bad luck could be coming with the flying stars.

It is not necessary for amateur practitioners to get involved in the technical details of flying star computations. But it is useful to have a reference table which enables readers to investigate the impact of the flying stars on their own feng shui, warning against the stars which bring serious bad luck, since these warn against ill health, loss and bad luck.

Please note that not every feng shui expert knows the flying stars. It is a very advanced and difficult branch of feng shui, and its effective practice requires knowledge of the method for working out the calculations as well as good judgmental and interpretative skills. Practising flying star feng shui that requires knowledge of the formulas as well as years of practical experience.

What are the flying stars?

The stars refer to the numbers 1 to 9 placed around the Lo Shu magic square. The numbers around the grid fly, ie they change over time. The way they change makes up the crux of this method of feng shui. Every day, month, year and every twenty-year period has its own arrangement of numbers around the square. Every number has its own meanings and tells the feng shui expert who knows how to interpret the numbers a great many things. For purposes of getting warnings, it is sufficient to monitor only the period and year stars.

The original nine sector Lo Shu square has the number 5 in the centre. In this square, the numbers have been arranged in such a way that the sum of any three numbers, taken vertically or horizontally or diagonally adds up to 15. This is the number of days it takes the moon to go from new moon to full moon. The numbers thus reflect the passage of time in a certain way. In flying star feng shui, the numbers move from grid to grid, and they are then interpreted according to what numbers are in which square. Each area of the grid represents a corner of a home with south placed on top, according to tradition. Use a compass and follow the instructions given on pages 36-7 to identify the actual corners of your home and turn the square accordingly.

The original Lo Shu square.

SOUTH

4	9	2
3	5	7
8	1	6

The period of 7

We are presently living the period of 7 which started in 1984 and does not end until the year 2003. During this period, the number 7 is deemed very lucky. The Lo Shu square for this period is shown to the left, and through an interpretation of the numbers it describes the fortunate and less fortunate sectors up to the year 2003.

During the period of 7, the bad luck star number 5 is located in the east. This is interpreted to mean that if the main door of your home is located in the east, you should be careful during this twenty year period which ends in the year 2003. It also means that those sleeping in bedrooms located in the east should be careful against being stabbed in the back. The bad luck star 2 is located in the south during this period. Lucky star numbers (and their corresponding corners) are marked with an *.

Warnings of loss and bad luck will be more accurate when investigations include the star numerals of the year as well as the month in question, and it is when two or all three star numerals are 5s or 2s or 5 or 2 in the same sector that loss due to extreme bad luck is certain during that month and year for people whose bedroom is in the sector where the bad numbers occur together! When you know the unlucky periods of your home, one way of countering the bad luck is to go for a holiday during that period, thereby 'running away' from the bad luck.

The period of 7 Lo Shu square.

SOUTH

*6	2	4
5	7	9
*1	3	*8

E ... W

N

The yearly reference table

This table shows where the stars 5 and 2 occur together in any year. Where 2s and 5s occur together that sector becomes dangerous, and anyone occupying rooms in those sectors would do well to move out of those rooms; or perhaps take a vacation. Be particularly careful when the star numerals 2 and 5 fall into the east sector. This is because this is the sector afflicted with the 5 in the twenty-year period flying star. Or in the south because this is where the number 2 is placed in the twenty-year period.

Year *	Star numeral 2 is in the	Star numeral 5 is in the
1997	southeast	west
1998	centre	northeast
1999	northwest	south*
2000	west	north
2001	northeast	southwest
2002	south *	east *
2003	north	southeast
2004		
(* based on the lunar year)		

Based on the reference table on the previous page, rooms in the south are prone to illness in 1999. In 2002, rooms in the south and east should be avoided, and in 2005, rooms in the east will be afflicted with bad luck such as illness, accidents and robbery.

The monthly reference table

The table below indicates the dangerous sectors during each of the twelve lunar months over the next five years. These are the sectors where the star numerals 2 and 5 are located during that month. Match where the star numerals 2 and 5 fall during the months indicated with those of the annual star numerals, and the twenty-year period star numerals.

If readers are generally guided by the unlucky directions given in the table below and take precautions, eg not sleep in the unlucky locations at the times indicated, they can avoid misfortunes. If the main door of a house happens to be located in an unlucky location during a particular month, then it is best to be out of the house during that month. One way of overcoming the unlucky star would be for the family to take a vacation.

| Year | Months | | | | | | | | | | | |
	1	2	3	4	5	6	7	8	9	10	11	12
1997	SW	E NW	SE** W	NE	S* NW	W N	NE SW	S* E*	N SE	SW	E* NW	SE W
1998	NE*	NW S*	W N	NE SW	S* E*	S* E*	N SE	SW	E NW	SE W	NE*	NW S
1999	NE SW	S* E*	N SE	SW	E* NW*	SE W	NE	NW* S*	W N	NE SW	S* E*	N SE
2000	SW	E* NW	SE W*	NE	NW S*	W N	NE SW	S* E*	N SE	SW	E* NW	SE W*
2001	NE	NW S*	W N	NE* SW*	S* E*	N SE	SW *	E* NW	SE W	NE	NW S*	W N
2002	SW NE	S* E*	N* SE	NW	E* NW	SE W	NE	S NW	N W	NE SW	E* S*	SE N
2003	SW*	E NW	SE* W	NE	S NE	N* W	SW NE	S E	SE N*	SW*	E NW	SE* W

(* based on the lunar months)

Formula School on directions

The best approach to directions and orientations is to use the compass formula on directions. This Pa Kua Lo Shu formula is potent and easy to use. It is also more exact and focused than using the generalized recommendations contained in the Yang Dwelling Classic.

The first step in using this method is to calculate your Kua number based on your date of birth and gender. The tables on the following pages

ANIMAL	WESTERN CALENDAR DATES	Year element	Kua for men	Kua for women
RAT (water)	Feb 18, 1912 - Feb 5, 1913	water	7	8
OX (earth)	Feb 6, 1913 - Jan 25, 1914	water	6	9
TIGER (wood)	Jan 26, 1914 - Feb 13, 1915	wood	5	1
RABBIT(wood)	Feb 14, 1915 - Feb 2, 1916	wood	4	2
DRAGON (earth)	Feb 3, 1916 - Jan 22, 1917	fire	3	3
SNAKE (fire)	Jan 23, 1917 - Feb 10, 1918	fire	2	4
HORSE (fire)	Feb 11, 1918 - Jan 31, 1919	earth	1	5
SHEEP (earth)	Feb 1, 1919 - Feb 19, 1920	earth	9	6
MONKEY(metal)	Feb 20, 1920 - Feb 7, 1921	metal	8	7
ROOSTER(metal)	Feb 8, 1921 - Jan 27, 1922	metal	7	8
DOG (earth)	Feb 28, 1922 - Feb 15, 1923	water	6	9
BOAR (water)	Feb 16th 1923 - Feb 4, 1924	water	5	1
RAT (water)	Feb 5th 1924 - Jan 23, 1925	wood	4	2
OX (earth)	Jan 24, 1925 - Feb 12, 1926	wood	3	3
TIGER (wood)	Feb 13, 1926 - Feb 1, 1927	fire	2	4
RABBIT (wood)	Feb 2, 1927 - Jan 22, 1928	fire	1	5
DRAGON (earth)	Jan 23, 1928 - Feb 9, 1929	earth	9	6
SNAKE (fire)	Feb 10, 1929 - Jan 29, 1930	earth	8	7
HORSE (fire)	Jan 30 1930 - Feb 16, 1931	metal	7	8
SHEEP (earth)	Feb 17 1931 - Feb 5 1932	metal	6	9
MONKEY (metal)	Feb 6, 1932 - Jan 25, 1933	water	5	1
ROOSTER (metal)	Jan 26, 1933 - Feb 13, 1934	water	4	2
DOG (earth)	Feb 14, 1934 - Feb 3, 1935	wood	3	3
BOAR	Feb 4, 1935 - Jan 23, 1936	wood	2	4
RAT (water)	Jan 24, 1936 - Feb 10, 1937	fire	1	5
OX (earth)	Feb 11, 1937 - Jan 30, 1938	fire	9	6
TIGER (wood)	Jan 31, 1938 - Feb 18, 1939	earth	8	7
RABBIT(wood)	Feb 19, 1939 - Feb 7, 1940	earth	7	8
DRAGON(earth)	Feb 8, 1940 - Jan 26, 1941	metal	6	9
SNAKE (fire)	Jan 27, 1941 - Feb 14, 1942	metal	5	1
HORSE (fire)	Feb 15, 1942 - Feb 4, 1943	water	4	2
SHEEP (earth)	Feb 5, 1943 - Jan 24, 1944	water	3	3
MONKEY (metal)	Jan 25 1944 - Feb 12 1945	wood	2	4
ROOSTER (metal)	Feb 13, 1945 - Feb 1, 1946	wood	1	5
DOG (earth)	Feb 2, 1946 - Jan 21, 1947	fire	9	6
BOAR (water)	Jan 22, 1947 - Feb 9, 1948	fire	8	7
RAT (water)	Feb 10, 1948 - Jan 28, 1949	earth	7	8
OX(earth)	Jan 29 1949 - Feb 16, 1950	earth	6	9
TIGER (wood)	Feb 17, 1950 - Feb 5, 1951	metal	5	1
RABBIT (wood)	Feb 6, 1951 - Jan 26, 1952	metal	4	2
DRAGON (earth)	Jan 27, 1952 - Feb 13, 1953	water	3	3
SNAKE (fire)	Feb 14, 1953 - Feb 2, 1954	water	2	4
HORSE (fire)	Feb 3, 1954 - Jan 23, 1955	wood	1	5
SHEEP (earth)	Jan 24, 1955 - Feb 11 1956	wood	9	6
MONKEY (metal)	Feb 12, 1956 - Jan 30 1957	fire	8	7
ROOSTER (metal)	Jan 31, 1957 - Feb 17, 1958	fire	7	8
DOG (earth)	Feb 18, 1958 - Feb 7, 1959	earth	6	9
BOAR (water)	Feb 8, 1959 - Jan 27, 1960	earth	5	1

ANIMAL	WESTERN CALENDAR DATES	Year element	Kua for men	Kua for women
RAT (water)	Jan 28, 1960 - Feb 14, 1961	metal	4	2
OX (earth)	Feb 15, 1961 - Feb 4, 1962	metal	3	3
TIGER (wood)	Feb 5, 1962 - Jan 24, 1963	water	2	4
RABBIT (wood)	Jan 25, 1963 - Feb 12, 1964	water	1	5
DRAGON (earth)	Feb 13, 1964 - Feb 1, 1965	wood	9	6
SNAKE (fire)	Feb 2, 1965 - Jan 20, 1966	wood	8	7
HORSE (fire)	Jan 21 1966 - Feb 8, 1967	fire	7	8
SHEEP (earth)	Feb 9 1967 - Jan 29, 1968	fire	6	9
MONKEY (metal)	Jan 30, 1968 - Feb 16, 1969	earth	5	1
ROOSTER (metal)	Feb 17, 1969 - Feb 5, 1970	earth	4	2
DOG (earth)	Feb 6 1970 - Jan 26, 1971	metal	3	3
BOAR (water)	Jan 27, 1971 - Feb 14 1972	metal	2	4
RAT (water)	Feb 15, 1972 - Feb 2, 1973	water	1	5
OX (earth)	Feb 3, 1973 - Jan 22, 1974	water	9	6
TIGER (wood)	Jan 23, 1974 - Feb 10, 1975	wood	8	7
RABBIT (wood)	Feb 11, 1975 - Jan 30, 1976	wood	7	8
DRAGON (earth)	Jan 31, 1976 - Feb 17, 1977	fire	6	9
SNAKE (fire)	Feb 18, 1977 - Feb 6, 1978	fire	5	1
HORSE (fire)	Feb 7, 1978 - Jan 27, 1979	earth	4	2
SHEEP (earth)	Jan 28, 1979 - Feb 15, 1980	earth	3	3
MONKEY (metal)	Feb 16, 1980 - Feb 4, 1981	metal	2	4
ROOSTER (metal)	Feb 5. 1981 - Jan 24, 1982	metal	1	5
DOG (earth)	Jan 25, 1982 - Feb 12, 1983	water	9	6
BOAR (water)	Feb 13, 1983 - Feb 1, 1984	water	8	7
RAT (water)	Feb 2, 1984 - Feb 19, 1985	wood	7	8
OX (earth)	Feb 20, 1985 - Feb 8, 1986	wood	6	9
TIGER (wood)	Feb 9, 1986 - Jan 28, 1987	fire	5	1
RABBIT (wood)	Jan 29, 1987 - Feb 16, 1988	fire	4	2
DRAGON (earth)	Feb 17, 1988 - Feb 5, 1989	earth	3	3
SNAKE (fire)	Feb 6, 1989 - Jan 26, 1990	earth	2	4
HORSE (fire)	Jan 27, 1990 - Feb 14, 1991	metal	1	5
SHEEP (earth)	Feb 15, 1991 - Feb 3, 1992	metal	9	6
MONKEY (metal)	Feb 4, 1992 - Jan 22, 1993	water	8	7
ROOSTER metal)	Jan 23, 1993 - Feb 9, 1994	water	7	8
DOG (earth)	Feb 10, 1994 - Jan 30, 1995	wood	6	9
BOAR (water)	Jan 31, 1995 - Feb 18, 1996	wood	5	1
RAT (water)	Feb 19, 1996 - Feb 6, 1997	fire	4	2
OX (earth)	Feb 7, 1997 - Jan 27, 1998	fire	3	3
TIGER (wood)	Jan 28, 1998 - Feb 15, 1999	earth	2	4
RABBIT (wood)	Feb 16, 1999 - Feb 4, 2000	earth	1	5
DRAGON (earth)	Feb 5, 2000 - Jan 23, 2001,	metal	9	6
SNAKE (fire)	Jan 24, 2001 - Feb 11, 2002	metal	8	7
HORSE (fire)	Feb 12, 2002 - Jan 31, 2003	water	7	8
SHEEP (earth)	Feb 1, 2003 - Jan 21, 2004	water	6	9
MONKEY (metal)	Jan 22, 2004 - Feb 8, 2005	wood	5	1
ROOSTER (metal)	Feb 9, 2005 - Jan 28, 2006	wood	4	2
DOG (earth)	Jan 29, 2006 - Feb 17, 2007	fire	3	3
BOAR (water)	Feb 18, 2007 - Feb 6, 2008	fire	2	4

give the Kua number of men and women born between 1912 and 2008.

Determining if you an east or west group person

If your Kua number is 1, 3, 4 or 9, you are an east group person and your detailed lucky and unlucky directions are as set down in the table below. These are applicable for both men and women. If your Kua number is either 5, 2, 6, 7 or 8 you are a west group person and your detailed lucky and unlucky directions are set down in the table at the bottom of the page.

East group directions

Kua NUMBERS	1	3	4	9
BEST DIRECTION	southeast	south	north	east
HEALTH DIRECTION	east	north	south	southeast
ROMANCE DIRECTION	south	southeast	east	north
PERSONAL GROWTH DIRECTION	north	east	southeast	south
UNLUCKY DIRECTION	west	southwest	northwest	northeast
FIVE GHOSTS DIRECTION	northeast	northwest	southwest	west
SIX KILLINGS DIRECTION	northwest	northeast	west	southwest
TOTAL LOSS DIRECTION	southwest	west	northeast	northwest

West group directions

Kua	5	5	2	6	7	8
NUMBERS	men	women	for ALL	for ALL	for ALL	for ALL
BEST DIRECTION	northeast	southwest	northeast	west	northwest	southwest
HEALTH DIRECTION	west	northwest	west	northeast	southwest	northwest
ROMANCE DIRECTION	northwest	west	northwest	southwest	northeast	west
PERSONAL GROWTH DIRECTION	southwest	northeast	southwest	northwest	west	northeast
UNLUCKY DIRECTION	east	south	east	southeast	north	south
FIVE GHOSTS DIRECTION	southeast	north	southeast	east	south	north
SIX KILLINGS DIRECTION	south	east	south	north	southeast	east
TOTAL LOSS DIRECTION	north	southeast	north	south	east	southeast

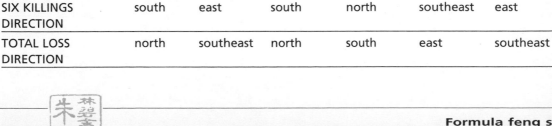

Using the tables

East group directions are east, south, north and southeast; west group directions are west, southwest, northwest and northeast. Depending on whether you are an east or west group person, your lucky directions bring you luck. Depending on your exact Kua number, each of these four directions will bring you a different kind of luck, and you should endeavour to orientate your home such that it has the main door facing your best direction as given in the appropriate table. Also, if you are an east group person, then all the west group directions will be inauspicious for you. How severe this bad luck is depends on your Kua number. If you are a west group person, the reverse is true.

Use the above tables to determine which specific direction you should activate for specific types of good luck, and also to determine how bad each of the opposing group directions are for you.

Please note, for instance, that if your main door faces your 'total loss' direction, it is likely that bad luck will befall you. Once you know what your unlucky directions are, you will be able to tell immediately whether the orientation of any particular house is lucky or unlucky for you. Simply check what direction the main front door faces (inside looking out).

Do remember, that in using the formula method on orientations, you must simultaneously guard against being hit by physical structures in the environment around you. Formula feng shui is powerful in bringing you good luck by harmonizing your personal chi with that of the environment; but it is not powerful enough to overcome the shar chi sent out by hostile physical structures like buildings, flyovers, and mountains. These can destroy all your good formula feng shui if they are threatening you.

When using formula methods, please note that the auspicious and inauspicious directions apply to the main door and not to the back door. The directions can be used to design the orientation of the home, as well as for each room. There are also other uses, dealt with in the later chapters.

Questions asked about the principles of feng shui

Q: Is the Pa Kua a religious or spiritual symbol?
A: I do not regard it as a religious symbol although I do believe there are spiritual connotations attached to the use of the Pa Kua as a protective symbol. I know that the Chinese like to have their Pa Kua blessed at the temple before installing it above their front door. For me, I use the Pa Kua only as a last resort. I do not attach any religious or spiritual connotations to it.

Q: What is the significance of the sigil of Saturn symbol formed by the Lo Shu arrangement of numbers?
A: It is a basis for speculating that feng shui as a practice is perhaps related to something similar in Hebrew and other cultures. I believe that the Chinese do not have exclusive knowledge of this environmental practice which promises so much. Other cultures probably have something similar to feng shui too. Only perhaps not so well documented.

Q: Are there other meanings and associations attached to the trigrams that you have not included in this book?
A: Oh definitely! If you read the *I Ching* carefully and study the multiple meanings of the trigrams and hexagrams, you will discover vast amounts of information. I refer you to the Richard Wilhelm translation as it is the most comprehensive. Do not try to study the *I Ching* from a simplified version. It is much too profound a text for frivolous reading.

Q: What if I cannot afford the changes necessary to improve my feng shui?
A: In situations that call for drastic changes to furniture or structures, use the formula methods of feng shui exclusively, unless what is wrong is due to the house directly facing a mountain. In this case there is nothing to do but to completely re-orientate the home. Otherwise just rearranging sitting and sleeping directions will have the most amazing good results.

Q: How do I determine the dragon and tiger sides of my home?
A: There are two methods. First, stand just inside your main door and look out. The land on your left is the dragon side while the land on your right is the tiger side.

The second method uses compass directions. Thus the east side of your house (where the morning sun shines) is the dragon side, while the west side is the tiger side. This is the side that gets the afternoon sun. Most practising feng shui masters use either one of these methods. It would be ideal if the left side also coincided with the east ... then you would not have to choose between the two methods.

Problems arise, however, when the left side is west and the right side is east. In such an instance, I would personally go with the compass direction method, although I do stress that there are feng shui experts I respect who disagree with me.

Q: How do I determine the shape of my house if it is totally irregular, and what if it has combinations of squares, circles and triangles? What perspective do I take – the layout plan or the elevation?
A: You can either artificially separate the parts and undertake your basic analysis accordingly, or, as recommended by most master practitioners, take a whole picture view of the entire house shape. Personally, I prefer the whole picture method since in this way all I need to do is address any problem of missing corners. The squares, circles and triangles indicate different element energies and you simply check the compass sector to see if the energies are in harmony according to where each of the shapes are located. As to whether you take the plan or elevation, my answer is both. Both perspectives are important, but if I have to choose which is more important, I would say it is the elevation.

Q: How do I know if the yin/yang balance of my home is correct? Do I need to keep rearranging my furniture every time the season changes?
A: When the energies of yin and yang are well balanced you will feel far more comfortable than if they are not. Some people call this instinctive. That may well be. However, my approach is that all yang dwellings of the living must have more yang than yin energy. The common problem is usually a shortage of yang energy. Or put another way, there is an excess of yin energy when your house is badly lit, dirty, cluttered, damp or altogeth-

er unhealthy smelling. Often, in such cases, merely opening the windows to let in the sunshine will clear the energies. Or open all the doors and windows occasionally to bring in fresh energies to replace the stale energies of a place that has been locked up all year. As to whether you need to respond to climatic changes of the season, the answer is yes, but you do not need to rearrange your furniture. Use lights, fireplaces and fans to increase or lessen yin and yang energies. As in the practice of anything, there is room for creativity and initiative.

Q: What should I do if my main door is hit by a poison arrow, and I find it impossible to reposition my door?
A: You can try to tilt it slightly. Even a few degrees could make a difference. Or create some kind of barrier between your door and the offensive structure opposite – a clump of heavy foliage trees is effective, or hang a protective Pa Kua.

Q: How do I know if I my home has bad feng shui?
A: You know something is wrong if you suffer a series of unfortunate occurrences shortly after moving into a new home. For instance, if your family take turns getting sick, or you lose your job for no good reason. Getting involved in an accident, or getting robbed … bad luck can sometimes be due to your own astrological chart seeing you through a bad period but if every person living in the same home seems to be suffering some manifestation of bad luck, it might be useful to check whether something harmful is affecting the feng shui of your home.

Usually these changes take place during the changeover of the feng shui periods: usually the lunar new year … and the next big period of change is due in the year 2003.

Q: What is your feeling about swimming pools?
A: I usually discourage the building of swimming pools in private homes. Having such a large body of water so close to the house can cause severe feng shui problems. Unless the land is very large, the danger of the pool overwhelming the house is very real indeed. It is also not easy to locate a pool correctly. If it happens to be sited on the right of the main door, for instance, the marriage of the residents becomes affected. And if it is located in the south, it will severely hurt the good name of the residents.

PART 2

Feng shui in and around your home

Harmonious layouts

Houses are said to have auspicious feng shui when all the elements and energies are in harmony with each other. Such houses live in the embrace of the celestial creatures – the turtle, phoenix, dragon and tiger – protected by mountains and soothed by a view of water, which also bring extreme good fortune. The five elements interact harmoniously and yin yang energies stay balanced at all times. Such houses are usually nestled into an auspicious corner of a hillside, shielded from poison arrows and benefiting from auspicious flows of the dragon's cosmic breath.

Inside, auspicious homes are designed to allow the sheng chi to meander harmoniously and slowly from room to room. The flow of chi is never allowed to become hostile. Nor is it allowed ever to stagnate or grow stale. In such a home, there will therefore not be any tight corners, straight corridors, nor doors in a straight line. Energies are kept vibrant with regular and proper maintenance.

House and room layouts will be auspicious if sheng chi is allowed to enter the home unencumbered, and then is allowed to flow from room to room in a meandering fashion. The main taboos of feng shui should be taken care of. Doors and windows should not cause chi to enter and rush out again. All poison arrows should either have been deflected or disarmed. Then, with good layout, you can be 70 per cent sure of enjoying good feng shui.

The principles of good home layout are:

1 The main door should not open into a crammed space directly facing a toilet, window, staircase, a pillar, corner or mirror.
2 The living room should be in the outer half of the house, nearer to the main door than the back door.
3 The dining and family rooms should be located in the centre part of the house. This is conducive to family harmony.
4 The kitchen should be in the inner half of the home, and nearer the back door than the front door.

Chi should ideally meander through a home so it is best not to have the main door and back door of the home aligned in a straight line.

A note on split floor levels and mezzanine floors

Generally, these are not favourable from a feng shui perspective. Split floor levels create confusion and uncertainty while a mezzanine floor is deemed to be a room with no foundation.

5 The toilets should be small and closed at all times, and doors into toilets should never directly face another door, a staircase, the bed or the dining table. Toilets should preferably not be located in the northwest and southeast of any home.

6 If the house has multiple levels, the dining area should be higher than the living room areas, and the sleeping areas should be at the highest level of the house. Multiple level homes are acceptable but split level homes are said to be unbalanced. They could cause severe financial loss.

7 There should not be any long corridors inside the home since long corridors create shar chi, and the result will be quarrels and misunderstandings in the home.

8 All structural columns and beams should be flush with the walls of the house. Exposed structural beams and corners create massive shar chi.

9 Doors and windows should not confront each other by being placed on opposite walls, facing each other.

10 Main doors, dining tables and work tables should never be placed directly under toilets. Toilets should be on top of each other to safeguard against this happening.

A word on toilets

In feng shui, the toilet is said to create foul breath which brings a multitude of bad luck and misfortune, with the exact nature of this bad luck depending on where the toilet is located. In the days of old China, almost all homes did not have toilets. The rich mandarins and the Royal household had baths and toilets brought in by slaves each day. The poorer classes and even the poorest of them all – the peasant class – would build their toilets some distance away from their dwellings. This reflected the basic belief that their places of sleeping, eating and working were never to be too near to where they cleaned themselves.

This particular tenet of feng shui is hard to follow in the modern day environment, and it is for this reason that I strenuously advise people to keep their toilets small and their toilet doors permanently closed. The later chapters contain additional taboos related to the placement of the toilet, and how bad luck caused by toilets can be alleviated to some extent.

Left: The toilet may be a small item in the home, but its significance is great because it has the potential to press down on good fortune.

Auspicious and inauspicious houses

When you live in a house with good feng shui you will find that you feel good about yourself. You will be healthy and energetic. Your career goes smoothly and there are opportunities for advancement. Incomes increase over time and all your relationships are smooth. Your mental attitude is positive. Your children do well at school, and both husband and wife find fulfilment in their lives and with each other.

When you are unfortunate enough to live in a house with bad feng shui, life is most unpleasant and negative. Everything and just about anything that can go wrong will. Opportunities are scarce, and even when they are present, you find you are unable to take advantage of them. There will be quarrels and misunderstandings, sickness and ill health. Accidents and mishaps happen all the time. Relationships between the family and with outsiders are not good. Incomes suffer and, in extreme cases, there is financial loss. Sickness can turn fatal. Children are listless and disobedient and both husband and wife find themselves sinking in a morass of problems and ill health. Life becomes quite terrible. Bad feng shui should be corrected as soon as possible.

Above: A house that is cradled by protective mountains has good feng shui.

Below: Living under a rock outcrop brings bad luck and misfortunes.

If you are suffering from bad feng shui, you can and must do something about it. Systematically go through your house and, one by one, identify the things that could be bringing you bad luck. Usually, it is not difficult to diagnose the problem areas and then rectify them.

Corrective feng shui need not be difficult. Often the solution can be simple. It is also not necessary to call in a feng shui expert since much feng shui is so easy you can do it yourself. Do not believe those who would have you think that feng shui is something spiritual, requiring psychic or intuitive powers. Feng shui is an ancient practice that is wonderfully scientific. Indeed, it is because it is so easy to practice that it has become so popular. Anyone can practice feng shui, including you.

The Chinese have used feng shui for thousands of years. It is part of our cultural tradition, and many western educated Chinese whose ancestors emigrated from China continued to practice feng shui. In Hong Kong and Taiwan, feng shui is a way of life. Business people would never move house without thoroughly checking the feng shui of their new home, and most of the old-timers prefer not to move, no matter how wealthy they get. This is because they are convinced their luck came from their original homes.

The new Governor of Hong Kong – CH Tung – was reported to prefer living in his own home and finding a new office because he was convinced the outgoing last British Governor's home and office had inauspicious feng shui.

In Singapore and Malaysia, feng shui is very popular with the Chinese population, and feng shui knowledge has also found its way to the West where it is accepted with considerable interest simply because it is so potent. When implemented correctly, feng shui guidelines do improve your luck – and it does not have to cost a lot.

Right: Business people in Hong Kong regard feng shui as a way of life.

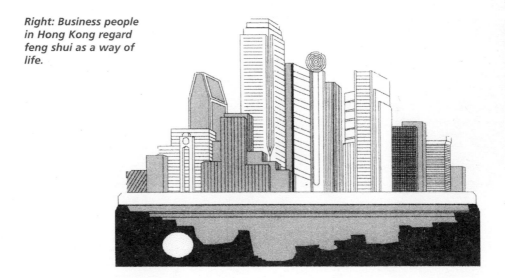

Orientations and directions

A large part of feng shui has to do with getting the orientations correct. Unless a house is positioned to make the maximum use of the surrounding topography, its feng shui cannot be maximized. This means placing the house, and tilting the direction it faces in a way that allows the house to have its surrounding land levels and elevations send auspicious chi towards the house rather than away from it.

It also means positioning the house to ensure its main door is adequately protected from the slings and arrows of any killing breath that may be present in the environment. The initial concern is to protect the home from bad feng shui.

Each of the eight main compass directions also emit various kinds of chi and the quality of this chi for the residents of the house is what brings them either great good fortune or loss and bad luck. Generally there are two ways of determining whether the direction of your house is considered auspicious or not. The first method is applicable to everyone and it is outlined here; the second method is based on the Pa Kua Lo Shu formula featured on pages 72-6, and is described overleaf.

The direction of the front door

The treatise on directions is contained in the *Yang Dwelling Classic*, and this book strongly advocates that the main door of a house – the mouth of the house – should face south. This advice was based on the attributes of this particular direction. Its element is fire and its trigram is li – both of which are indications of strong yang energy.

The crimson phoenix brings opportunities for advancement.

The south is considered to be the source of many good things in feng shui symbolism. As such, if your house does face south and you are backed by a hill or some higher land which gives you support, then your direction feng shui can be described as generally favourable. Also, by facing south, your home will automatically comply with the other feng shui classical configuration, which recommends that houses face the place of the crimson phoenix (see page 26) thereby benefiting from the many opportunities for advancement that this celestial creature brings. The place of the phoenix is the south.

There are other recommendations for directions that are auspicious and those to avoid. Certain schools of feng shui strenuously warn against facing the southwest and describe this as the entrance to hell. Personally, I do not subscribe to this particular ruling since this is the direction of the matriarch and is the place of the trigram kun, which is, of course, regarded as the opposite of the trigram chien, the patriarch.

The southwest is the sector that is the most yin in terms of energy and perhaps it is this interpretation that has led to advice against doors facing southwest. My own home faces this direction and has done for the last twenty years and I do not believe it has caused me any problems. The southwest happens to be favourable for me, but I also hang two crystal chandeliers, one just inside and the other just outside the door. Those of you with front doors facing the southwest, the south and the northeast can do the same.

The northwest is designated as the place of the patriarch. If your main door faces this ultimate yang direction, keep your main door open for some hours at least once a week to welcome in the energy which is said to come from heaven. The northwest is the direction of the trigram chien, which symbolizes heaven.

A chandelier in the home

A chandelier introduces precious yang energy that balances the yin of this direction, but it also creates vital element harmony. Light, being of the element fire, creates the element earth, which is the intrinsic energy of this sector. I am a great advocator of the crystal chandelier, and if you can afford it I strongly recommend that you invest in one to hang in the middle of your living room, too. More than anything, the chandelier creates excellent vibrations for the home, attracting money and success luck to each and every member of the family. Crystal chandeliers bring even greater luck if their location coincides with either the fire or earth corners of the home or of the room; these are the south, the southwest or the northeast corners.

Chandeliers are excellent feng shui for main doors.

The Pa Kua Lo Shu formula

According to the Pa Kua Lo Shu formula, the north-south alignments are believed to be either extremely good or extremely bad. If you are an east group person (see pages 75-6), you benefit enormously from having your main door face either north or south. However, if the Pa Kua Lo Shu ormula designates you a west group person, this alignment will cause you a great deal of problems, especially when the door faces north, the place of the danger trigram kan.

Roads and driveways

We have already noted the bad feng shui of inauspicious junctions that create hostile killing breath; of straight roads that bring death and misfortune, and of flyovers and over passes that represent harmful approaches to any home or building (see pages 53-7). There are, however, other external features nearer to home that also cause inauspicious feng shui. Here are some of the more common of these problems which need bearing in mind at all times.

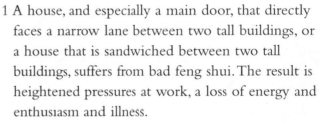

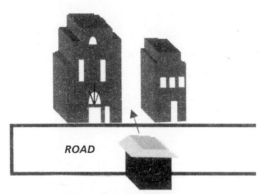

Directly facing a narrow lane caused by tall buildings is also bad feng shui.

1 A house, and especially a main door, that directly faces a narrow lane between two tall buildings, or a house that is sandwiched between two tall buildings, suffers from bad feng shui. The result is heightened pressures at work, a loss of energy and enthusiasm and illness.

    If you cannot move out, the best cure is to re-orientate your main door if you are facing this narrow lane, and to install a bright light above the roof of your house if you are sandwiched between two buildings. This raises the chi and should alleviate the situation. Another solution is to place a large concave mirror on the roof that will symbolically deflect the image of adjoining buildings.

Being sandwiched between tall buildings brings bad luck.

2 A house, and especially the main door, that directly faces a dead end, or worse yet, confronts a circular driveway that resembles a Chinese tomb, can result in residents frequently falling ill. There will also be a great deal of disharmony. Children will suffer and become difficult to control and excessive yin energy gives rise to ill tempers, quarrels and immense bad luck in all endeavours. Facing a dead end usually means no way out. The solution is to paint your door a bright red, install two bright gate lights at least

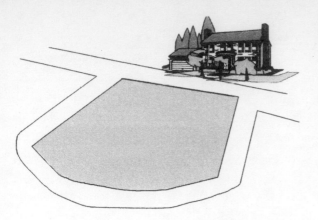

Facing this sort of road arrangement is like facing a tomb because of the shape of the road, and the way the road curves round. Grow a clump of trees as shown.

3 m (3 yd) above ground level, and plant a clump of trees to block out the view of the offending road layout.

3   Driveways should never be a straight road pointing directly at the main door. This is as bad as the T-junction and is, in fact, similar in effect. Driveways should preferably curve *towards* the main door, but not *at* the door. Circular driveways are regarded as auspicious, but they really should be circular and not merely curved in the shape of a knife. Circular driveways with a fountain in the centre are said to be especially auspicious. Driveways with a single gate are preferable to having two gates, unless yours is an enormous estate. Having two gates fronting an average size residential house could give rise to imbalance and money flowing outwards. It is not recommended.

4   Driveways should be level. When the road is too steep going down into the house, the feng shui is faulty. When the road goes upwards, the feng shui is not as bad, but it is not as good as having the driveway level with the outside approach road.

5   Driveways can and should always be enhanced with lights. Keeping a pair of lights on either side of the driveway allows the energy to stay balanced. Driveways should also be of even width. Those that narrow inwards or narrow outwards create imbalance and result in bad luck as

This driveway is inauspicious.

It should be curved, or circular, like this.

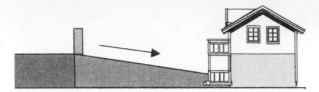

A driveway that slopes downwards towards the house is not recommended. This also means that the house is below road level. Better to have the driveway at the same level as the road outside.

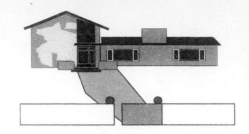

A driveway that narrows outwards is bad luck.

opportunities cannot ripen fruitfully and there is difficulty in saving. Whatever income comes into the home goes right out again. The best driveways are parallel to the front door. Better yet, they should appear to meander towards the main door.

Fences and gates

The boundary of the home demarcates the parameters of energy that swirl around the home. There are therefore important feng shui guidelines pertaining to fences and gates that should be observed. These have to do with levels, shapes, materials used and design patterns.

1 Any fence around the home should ideally be the same height all round, but especially so where it flanks the front gate. If one side of the fence is higher than the other it is said to be out of balance. It is not auspicious to have a fence built in this way and fortunes may fluctuate and not hold steady.

2 Solid fences are better than see-through fences. Hence brick walls and wooden fences are preferable to grilled or chain link fencing. Having said this, experts do advise the use of element analysis when designing boundaries. The south, southwest and northeast walls are luckier when built with bricks or concrete. The boundaries on the west, northwest and north should ideally be made of steel or other metal. The fences on the east and southeast should be made of wood.

3 Sensitivity should be used when designing grills and wooden panelled fences. The things to avoid are pointed arrows – either pointing inwards (which hurt you) or pointing outwards (which hurt your neighbours). In fact, avoid spikes altogether unless they are pointing upwards. Wooden fences should avoid having crosses or downward pointing arrows as these tend to hurt the house.

4 Gates should follow the guidelines offered for fences. Choose the materials according to where the main gate is located.

Cross designs are not encouraged as these emit shar chi towards the house. Pointed diamond-shaped designs are also not encouraged. Anything pointed creates shar chi.

The main door

Having dealt with the most common external structures that can harm the feng shui of your main door, it is equally important to examine placements and objects that can cause feng shui problems to the main door from inside the home. Articles can work against the harmony within the home either by blocking sheng chi from coming into the home, or preventing chi from flowing unencumbered through the home. Or they send shar chi shooting directly at the main door.

The main door is one of the most important features of feng shui practice and its feng shui should be safeguarded at all costs. The orientations of the door should be auspicious. Also nothing should be allowed to harm the main door. Feng shui is clear about this – get the main door right, make it auspicious, and 80 per cent of your feng shui is assured. On the other hand, if the feng shui of the main door is flawed, the effect is magnified and bad luck caused is severe. Here are important ground rules to observe with respect to the feng shui of your door.

The main door and toilets placement

The main door should not have a toilet placed directly above it on the upper level. This causes very severe bad luck. So do make certain that bathrooms and toilets on the first floor level are not directly above the foyer

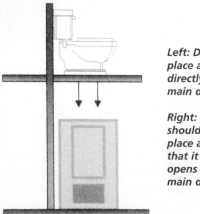

Left: Do not place a toilet directly over the main door.

Right: Nor should you place a toilet so that it directly opens onto the main door.

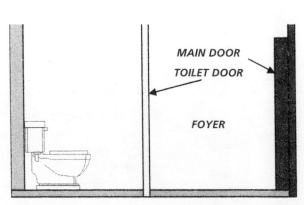

MAIN DOOR

TOILET DOOR

FOYER

and inadvertently hurting your main door. If it is, change the location of the door or use another door as the main door. If this is not possible, try not to use the toilet upstairs, and place a high voltage light on the ceiling of the foyer. This clears the bad energy to some extent.

The main door should also not open and directly face a toilet. If it does, then any good fortune entering your home will get flushed away. This is a particularly harmful arrangement, and the best way to handle it is to keep the toilet closed at all times. If the toilet door is not face to face with the main door, you might want to consider placing a mirror on the toilet door. This symbolically makes the toilet disappear.

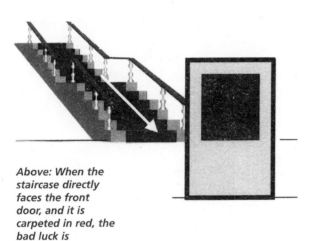

Above: When the staircase directly faces the front door, and it is carpeted in red, the bad luck is extremely severe.

Right: When there is one staircase going up and another going down, the effect is very unbalanced. Nothing will succeed in such a household. Here the best solution would be to create some kind of barrier using either a new partition if the foyer is wide enough or place a screen between the main door and the staircase.

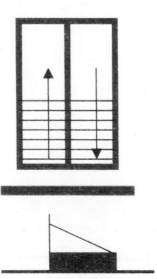

The main door and staircases

The main door should never face a staircase directly. Whether the staircase is going up or down, this is not an auspicious arrangement, and the longer the staircase, the more harm it does to the home.

Arrangements where the staircase directly faces the main door are very common in the West, and especially in Britain where many London town houses have this unfortunate feature. For many, however, the staircase only half faces the front door. In some cases I have noticed that the last three steps are cleverly turned away from the front door. This is an excellent feng shui cure. Chinese restaurants operating in London that have this feature deal with it by building a very neat barrier between the main door and the staircase, thereby making certain their business does not suffer from this bad feng shui. When all else fails, hanging a wind chime in the centre of the wall just above the door on the outside, and installing a bright light, helps to disperse some of the bad chi that has been created by the staircase. Nevertheless, the best solution of all is to create a barrier that blocks out the view of the staircase altogether.

The main door and mirrors

Almost every feng shui expert I have consulted agrees with me about having a mirror directly facing and reflecting the main door. It is believed that when the main door is reflected in a big wall mirror, not only does the luck of the household start to diminish, but the health of the head of the household is also said to suffer. In general, mirrors must be used with great care. My advice is that you should examine what is being reflected in the mirror.

Where the mirror reflects the main door, any good fortune coming in through the mouth of the house goes right out again, almost instantly. I have suffered from this oversight. I had placed a huge wall mirror on one wall of my dining room (this is an auspicious feature). Unfortunately, I had overlooked the fact that although my dining room was at least 10 m (30 ft) from my main door, because the mirror was so big and it directly faced the main door, it was reflected in the mirror. Alas, this was bad news indeed as all my good fortune would fly out of the door inside the mirror! Hurriedly, I installed a big screen between the mirror and the door, thereby saving my feng shui.

In case readers start getting paranoid about decorative mirrors placed near the main door, please note that unless the mirror is directly reflecting the door, the mirror does not do any harm.

Corners and main doors

It seems hard to believe that there are houses and apartments built with corners, pillars and sharp edges directly facing the main door. These structures represent poison arrows that hit the door from inside the house. They do no good for the residents, and significantly represent

Czar Nicholas's staircase

The most awful example of how lethal a staircase can be is the grand staircase that directly faces the main door of the palace in Saint Petersburg that was occupied by Czar Nicholas and his family. The palace is now being used as a tourist attraction where there are nightly performances of folk dancing, which is how I came to see and know about it. Here the main door is very big and grand. But the staircase is even bigger and grander. It starts not more than 2 m (6 ft) from the door, and it goes straight up for two levels before splitting into two, on the left and right. In the old days this staircase was probably covered with red carpet, signifying blood. Such a staircase is the most lethal of poison arrows. I often wonder if it is more than a coincidence that Czar Nicholas and his entire family were murdered – a situation described in feng shui as chueh ming – total loss.

A plant positioned in front of a protruding corner helps to mask the potential harmful chi that will emanate from the corner.

deadly bad luck. Every effort should be made to counter the effect by placing bushy or creeper plants to soften the edges of the sharp corner facing the door. In the illustration opposite, the wall creates the corner and this has been dealt with by the strategic positioning of a plant. The same solution can be applied to a pillar or a protruding corner.

The main door and other doors

When three or more doors are placed directly in a straight line, the feng shui created is considered lethal. The only thing that is worse is when one of the doors is the main door and the other is the back door. This is a feng shui taboo known to almost every practising feng shui amateur. If you are unfortunate enough to have this feature in your home, I strongly advise you to place some kind of barrier in front of the middle door to force the fast flowing shar chi to slow down, curve round the barrier, and in the process transform into something less harmful. This barrier can be any kind of partitioning or decorative screen.

Hanging a wind chime or a pair of flutes is also a solution, but it is not as effective as placing a screen. Whatever action you decide on, you should do it fast since this is one of the more dangerous of feng shui taboos. To make sure that at least the middle door stays shut, so that the three doors are never open all at the same time, it is also a good idea to fit an automatic door closer.

Above: If you have three doors in a row, place a screen between two of them to slow down the rush of chi.

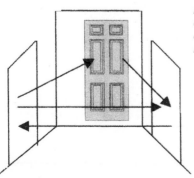

Left: When three doors open onto each other, quarrels may occur regularly.

Slowing down chi
Corridors are bad news and the longer they are, the more serious will be their ill effects. If your room is placed at the end of a long corridor, the effect is like being at the end of a T-junction where the killing breath rushes headlong at you. The best way of handling corridors is to place objects along the corridor that slow down the chi flowing through. Plants, for example, will slow down the chi, as will a wind chime or hollow bamboo stems tied with red thread.

If the three doors end in a door leading to a bedroom, the result is that bad energy comes into the bedroom, adversely affecting the occupants. It is always a good idea to keep the bedroom far away from the main door. One solution is to place a screen divider between the bedroom and the main door, but if there isn't enough space, hang a curtain, plastic blinds, or wooden shutters – anything that can effectively create a barrier.

When there are two doors directly facing each other, they are said to be in confrontation with each other. There will be likelihood of the occupants being impatient with each other.

When there are three doors together and they form a triangle, the indication is that quarrels and misunderstandings will be a regular feature of the domestic scene. The way to counter the negative energy here is to hang a wind chime in the centre of the triangle, successfully dissolving the vortex of fierce energies and reducing conflicts within the household. Placing a strong light in the corridor within sight of the three doors is another effective way of overcoming the bad energy.

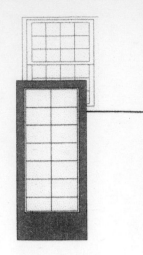

When a main door directly faces a window sheng chi flows in and out again ...

Main doors and windows

Main doors that directly face windows on the opposite wall have a hard time holding on to any sheng chi coming into the home. Such a windows causes good fortune to float right out again. It is for this reason that feng shui experts usually recommend against having openings on opposite walls. Windows should always be on the walls that are on either side of the door, keeping the opposite wall solid. This ensures that chi which comes into the home has a chance to settle and accumulate, thereby benefiting the residents.

This guideline is especially significant when the windows in your home are floor length since this, in effect, makes them into doors. Remember that the idea of feng shui is to capture the vital sheng chi, or good breath, and having doors opposite each other is not the way to do it.

Structural features to avoid

There are four major structural features to look out for in the interior of any house or apartment. Because they are structural, every home has these features. But how they are placed in relation to the main door, and where they are located in relation to the working, sitting and sleeping areas of occupants have feng shui significance. So look out for these features, assess their impact on your health and luck, and, if necessary, introduce some innovative remedies that can successfully camouflage their presence.

Structural overhead beams

These cause a great deal of problems as heavy, exposed beams send out shar chi from above. In most cases, beams are angular and massive, and they have sharp edges that create bad luck, weighing down immovably on anyone unfortunate enough to be working, sitting or sleeping beneath them. The bad luck created can be as harmless as headaches and migraines or as serious as a severe illness or financial loss. Either camouflage such beams, or move from under them, or better yet, do both. If you live in a ground floor flat of a multi-level apartment block, just imagine say twenty floors of the same structural beam hitting at you while you sleep or work.

The solution for deflecting and dissolving the bad energies created by such beams is to install a false ceiling. This is the most effective solution since the beam actually disappears from view. But whether or not you are able to use this method depends on your budget and on the height of your ceiling. Another, simpler, solution is to place objects like creeper plants and decorative frills on the beams' edges. Either of these soften the edges, even though the heaviness of a load above you will remain.

Imagine sitting under a heavy overhead beam like this. It is like having a heavy load hang over you. Softening the edges with creeper plants can help, but not a lot. It might be better to hang bamboo stems tied with red thread to defeat the shar chi of such beams.

Another method is to hang a large wind chime or a curved knife on the beam. This works for beams located in the east and southeast sectors. In the southwest and the northeast corners, hanging a pair of hollow bamboo stems tied with red thread (see page 63) also negates the beams' shar chi.

While heavy structural beams cause serious feng shui problems, other exposed non-structural or decorative features that appear as part of ceilings also cause problems. The rustic look, for instance, can have overhead girders and rafters, and decorative plaster ceilings that sport angular designs can be a problem, too. The best ceilings are those that are flat with nothing protruding outwards and downwards.

Protruding corners

Corners are as problematic as overhead beams, and as common. Almost all homes have these badly designed engineering requirements which can so easily be camouflaged at the drawing stage, but which usually are not. I have been told that protruding corners and overhead beams are a result of budget constraints. Such houses are simply cheaper, and easier to build. But these features cause bad feng shui and if your home has these protruding corners, I advise you to try and camouflage them.

If the sharp edges of the corners are not directly pointing at your main door, or your sleeping or working places, you escape the killing shar chi being sent out by the edges. But if you are unfortunate enough to be in the path of these negative energies, your luck will suffer, causing you stress in your work and love life. Your health will also suffer.

There are three excellent methods for dealing with protruding corners and these are:

◆ Hang a large wind chime just in front of the edge of the corner.
◆ Hang hollow bamboo stems tied with red thread.
◆ Place a potted plant that has leafy foliage to camouflage the sharp edge.

Use a combination of methods around the house if you wish. Feng shui solutions need not look ugly if you are creative. If you use plant therapy, though, please remember to throw out the plant as soon as it shows signs of fading (see also pages 62–3). Believe me, even the healthiest of plants cannot live long when being hit daily by the shar chi of a sharp corner. So change your plant frequently or use a fake potted plant. These are effective feng shui cures. Never use dried or dead plants as they emit yin energy and you will merely be exchanging one problem for another.

Never use plants in your bedroom because plants in the bedroom do not bring good luck. Instead, they tend to sap your energy. The best method here is the bamboo stem method.

Above: A square pillar with its corners shaved off softens the harmful effects that such a pillar can have on its surroundings.

Stand alone pillars and columns

Stand alone pillars and columns are also a common occurrence in homes because they represent a saving on construction costs. Unfortunately, they have the same effect as protruding corners except that the chances of being hurt by these pillars is considerably increased since because they stand alone there are four sharp corners sending out shar chi – the killing breath. These columns also tend to be structural and so carry the weight of the building.

Round pillars are not as bad as square ones, but they also represent obstacles, so I strongly recommend that you try not to have pillars in your home unless you are so wealthy and rich that you have the means to invest in expensive feng shui cures.

In public buildings like hotels and shopping arcades, massive square pillars have negative impact on business unless these pillars are suitably and beautifully camouflaged. Look at the stunning pillars that adorn the foyers of the Shangri La Hotels of the Far Eastern cities, for instance. They are all beautifully camouflaged so that the edges never hurt anyone, and definitely they do not hurt their business. To start with, these pillars have their edges cut off so that the square becomes octagonal (see illustrations to the left).

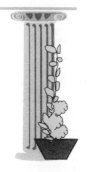

Above: Round decorative columns like this one are not as harmful as square columns. But it is good feng shui to place a potted plant at its base.

The best way of dealing with stand alone pillars is to wrap the whole pillar with mirror, making the pillar symbolically disappear. The other method is to use plant therapy, surrounding the pillars with potted plants to soften the edges.

Staircases

These are purveyors of chi from one level of the home to the other, and the nature of their construction has serious feng shui consequences. The types of staircases that bring bad luck are:

1 Spiral staircases, which are said to resemble a corkscrew. If they are located in the middle of the home, they are described as a corkscrew boring into the heart of the home; and if they are carpeted in red, they are described as the result of a bleeding heart. These colourful descriptions tell their own story. Do shun spiral staircases, I have seen them cause serious personal grief to several families.

2 Cantilevered staircases which have open, rather than solid spaces between them, are inauspicious because luck leaks out even as it climbs to the upper levels. Always go for solid staircases, and never carpet your staircases in red. This is not a good colour to attract chi upstairs.

Place staircases in the central one third of the home, but at the side rather than right at the centre. A staircase at the centre of the home resembles an injured household and consequently family unity and family luck are adversely affected. Sometimes the bad luck of such a feature can be lethal. If you have this feature, the staircase should be absolutely solid in which case it will do no harm, but if it is cantilevered, the effect is most serious. Place a powerful light from the top of the ceiling shining down on the staircase to ward off the ill-effect and keep the light turned on as much as possible.

Never allow a staircase to face the main or back doors without correcting it. Nor should it face the door of the master bedroom or lead up directly to the toilet door. These are extremely inauspicious arrangements, and should be dealt with by placing some sort of barrier between to dispel the bad energy created by the disharmonious meeting of these structures.

If there is insufficient space to place a barrier, then the orientation of the first three steps of the staircase should be altered so that the whole staircase is perceived to have changed direction.

Feng shui decorating finishing touches

Taking note of the major feng shui taboos that apply to house interiors saves you a great deal of trouble. Once you become totally familiar with the objects, designs, colours and styles that can inadvertently create bad luck for your home, you will find feng shui practice becomes second nature.

Pictures

Paintings of landscapes such as mountains and rivers are excellent from a feng shui perspective, especially when hung correctly. Always display mountains behind where you sit, and water views in front of you. Mountains offer symbolic support. A print of Mount Everest represents support from a very high mountain, and would be excellent when hung in the study or work office of the family patriarch or matriarch.

Paintings of good fortune flowers like the peony, chrysanthemum, orchid and magenta (to name a few), will all be auspicious. When these are featured on other artistic products like ceramic vases, cloisonné boxes or pottery, they create harmonious energies for the home. The rule is to avoid anything that appears threatening.

Be careful when buying paintings for the home. Apart from wild animals, also avoid abstract art that contains many sharp points. And do avoid sad looking paintings. Picasso's 'Weeping Woman', for instance, may be great in a museum, but is absolutely horrible to hang in the home. Also avoid paintings or prints of wrinkled looking old men and women. These so-called character paintings create unhealthy energy. Instead, go for paintings that inspire, that look happy and which suggest wealth and prosperity. One of the best feng shui objects to have on display in the home is a family portrait where every member of the family looks happy. This is one sure way of keeping the family together.

Harmful objects that are best avoided include paintings and ceramic creations of wild animals. I have seen exquisitely made

Hanging a painting of a fierce animal in the home is a big NO.

ceramic leopards and tigers that look deliciously ferocious and would have loved to display these beautiful big cats in my living room. But I also know that inviting one of these wild animals into my home is simply asking for trouble. The energy exuded is the killing breath, especially if displayed in the bedroom. In the same vein, I do advise you to throw out souvenirs of big game hunting: deer antlers and tiger skin rugs are taboo from a feng shui perspective.

Soft furnishings

Inappropriate designs should be avoided in all your soft furnishings and other design details within the home. Always avoid motifs that are sharp, angular or threatening choosing instead designs that have curves, are rounded, and seem to be flowing. In feng shui, it does seem that art nouveau is to be preferred over art deco!

Grill designs that feature spikes, plaster ceilings that have angular edges, lamp shades that look threatening, chairs that feature deadly sharp corners – all these are design features that should have no place in a feng shui home. It is especially dangerous to intro-duce designs that suggest arrows, points, triangles and anything else that seems hostile, threatening or fierce.

A curved design is preferable when choosing a motif for interior decor.

A pointed design should be avoided.

Colour combinations

The feng shui of colours and colour combinations can be so easily incor-porated into the decor of a home that it seems sensible to do so. In feng shui, no single colour is good or bad. Instead, every person or type of home will have their own more auspicious, or less auspicious colours, or combi-nations of colours.

For individuals, there are two ways to investigate the colours that do or do not work for you. Start with your date of birth. Go to the tables that list out the elements for a hundred years on pages 73-4. Scroll through the table to find out your year element and your animal element. If these two elements are friendly to each other – one producing the other – then use

Choosing a design motif

It is best to choose from a wide range of auspicious design motifs. Use the five elements to give you clues as to what are the most appropriate designs for each corner of the room, and design your rooms to benefit you. You can do this by checking the year element of your date of birth given on pages 73-4. Then look for motifs that reflect your year element. Or select something that belongs to the element that produces your element.

For example, if you were born in the year 1945, your year element would be wood, so a wood design - plants, for instance - or water would be excellent to use for your living room and bedrooms. Shown to the right are examples of motifs of each of the five elements to give you an idea of the choices available. I have very prosperous friends who, having discovered the motif that best works for them then use them all their lives, and they always succeed at what they do, at home or in business.

What you should strenuously try to avoid is to inadvertently select design motifs that

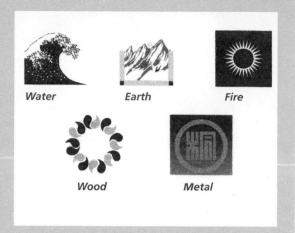

Water   Earth   Fire

Wood   Metal

symbolize the element that destroys your intrinsic energy: the energy of the element that represents your year of birth. For example, if the element that rules your year of birth is metal then having sunflowers and sun motifs all over the home will be sure to cause you harm. This is because excessive fire destroys metal. Fire, in small quantities, however, enhances the value of metal. Thus also be aware of balance. Fire is excellent for anyone whose birth year is of the earth element.

OCHRE FOR SOUTHWEST	RED FOR SOUTH	GREEN FOR SOUTHEAST
METALLIC FOR WEST		GREEN FOR EAST
METALLIC FOR NORTHWEST	BLUE FOR NORTH	OCHRE FOR NORTHEAST

these two elements to determine the colour combinations that correctly reflect your ruling elements.

The second method is governed by your year element, and using that to identify the colours that best suits you. Work through the colour combinations based on the colours of the five elements outlined in the box, to the left.

An excellent method of determining colours for the different rooms of your home is to determine which compass corner each of the major rooms occupies and then use a colour scheme that has the relevant element prevailing. Thus green should be dominant in the east and southeast, red should dominate in the south and so on, also as outlined in the box, at the foot of page 103.

A good way of determining the compass corners of the home is to superimpose the Lo Shu grid which divides the home into nine equal squares or rectangles. The compass direction is then taken from the centre of the home. Taking the compass reading from the heart of the home results in a more accurate reading of the compass. From this reading, determine the compass direction of each of the major rooms. The colours you decide for decorating each corner of your home can be used on the walls in the form of paint or wallpaper; on soft furnishings in the form of curtains, sofa covers, bedspreads and cushion covers, and on the floor on carpets. But do not over indulge. If you have everything in red, for example, or blue or black, you will have created extremely bad feng shui since your rooms will be excessively yin or too yang – both of which situations are not good.

Getting the feng shui right for important corners of the home is vital. It is no use setting out to improve your feng shui if you do not know what or where to focus your attention. The major rooms requiring your undivided attention in terms of feng shui are the foyer where the main door is

Colours for the home

Fire (south)
All shades of red, yellow, and orange. These are yang colours which offer excellent support for ochre and other earth colours, but which are deadly when combined with white.

Water (north)
All shades of blue and black. This is a very yin colour, but it offers superb productive energies for the wood colours of greens and browns. The water shades are extremely hostile when combined with red since water extinguishes fire so avoid them.

Wood (east, southeast)
All shades of greens and browns. These are also yang colours that denote growth. They are excellent when combined with red, enhancing the red tremendously. They are less suitable for the earth colours.

Metal (west, northwest)
All shades of gold, silver and white. These are colours that have very powerful yang energies. They combine extremely well with water colours, and a special water colour is purple which combines exceptionally well with silver. Metal colours should never be placed together with wood colours. This combination kills growth, and is best avoided.

Earth (southwest, centre and northeast)
All shades of ochre, beige and browns. The earth colours work well with the metallic colours. Earth colours are yin colours, and they cause havoc when combined with water colours, which are also yin. The two yin energies cause excess that spells trouble. Black should therefore not be combined with earth colours.

located, the living room, the dining room and the master bedroom. The practice also tends to be rather male orientated so that it is the auspicious directions of the senior male that must benefit most from good feng shui. This does not mean only following the formula given on pages 72–6 but also involves getting the northwest correct (see box, opposite).

The importance of the northwest

This is the universally designated corner that belongs to the family patri-arch. It is of the metal element, so the best colour scheme for this corner would be white. The northwest should also not house the kitchen, the storeroom or the garage; and most especially the toilet. If it does, it will detract from the luck of the patriarch, since these are excessively yin rooms.

Keep the northwest alive with yang energy if you wish to enhance the standing, prestige and wealth of the patriarch. Energize this corner with metal bells and wind chimes. Place your television here if you wish. The moving images suggest precious yang energy.

Energizing the living room

The living room is where the family entertains. It is also where the family gathers so good feng shui in the living room affects the harmony, prosperity and success of the family. This is thus the best room in the house to energize. To design an auspicious living room, it is important that the shape be regular, that it be well lighted, and that furniture is carefully laid out.

A square or rectangular-shaped living room is the most auspicious. If the main door opens into the living room, try not to have it face a window directly opposite. Having a window immediately by its side is also not recommended. Nor is it wise to place any tall cabinet or chairs just next to or near the main door. This seriously impairs the feng shui of both the living room and the house since the main door is affected.

Floor materials and designs should also be regular. I dislike the crazy marble floors so popular with housing developers where floors are laid out with broken marble or terrazzo tiles. They impart a sense of disorder and confusion to the living room. If you have such floors, I suggest you have your living room retiled or cover it with a solid colour carpet.

Smooth floors are preferable to rough floors. In the living room, where the family entertains their guests, pebbled stoned and other uneven floors are not suitable. They suggest imbalance, obstacles and a rough ride through life. Instead, opt for the smooth surface of a well-polished floor if you want good feng shui.

If you have patterns on your floors caused by wooden, parquet or carpet designs, do make sure that the lines created do not form harmful crosses and triangles. Straight lines that run across the room from the door

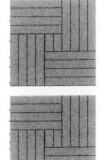

Above: Regular designs on the floor are to be preferred over haphazard designs.

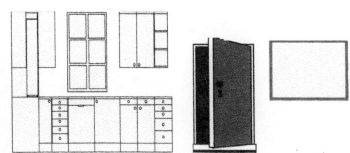

Left: The main door illustrated here is not auspicious. It opens into the living room but the proximity of so much tall furniture adversely affects the energy entering the home.

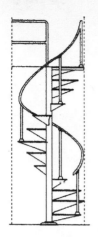

Spiral staircases act like a cork screw, creating negative energy.

inwards are said to draw the chi into the home. But if the lines seem to be flowing out, then chi will likewise flow outwards. It is probably best to try to avoid having patterns at all.

In the living room, ceilings can energize your feng shui, or they can create havoc. Modern living rooms today sport plaster ceilings that come with many different designs. Many of these designs have cornices, and as long as they have rounded edges they do not cause harm to your feng shui. What you need to guard against, though, are ceilings that come with rectangular designs that have sharp multiple edges on each of the four sides. It would be better to go for ceiling designs that do not have protrusions or troughs. It is acceptable to have a recessed area in the centre from where you can hang the ultimate feng shui energizer – a crystal chandelier.

Slanted ceilings, or ceilings that have exposed rafters, can seriously affect the feng shui of the living room. Deal with these rafters as you would an exposed overhead beam (see page 97). If you have a slanted ceiling, correct the imbalance of the room, raising the chi by placing lights along the side where the ceiling is low.

Spiral staircases in the living room are also not an especially good idea. Many old apartments have them leading up to a mezzanine floor. While this looks good from an interior decorative viewpoint, in reality, spiral staircases create negative energy and are not auspicious in the home. If you have such a staircase, try to change it to a regular solid staircase.

Sofa and coffee table arrangements in the living room are auspicious when they generally form a regular overall shape. L-shaped arrangements are not recommended because corners are created which, of course, cause

Energize the east and southeast with plants. These are the corners ruled by the wood element, and the objects that are most effective for activating the wood element are healthy growing plants.

Energize the north, east and southeast with water features if you want to get rich. Aquariums and miniature fountains will do very nicely.

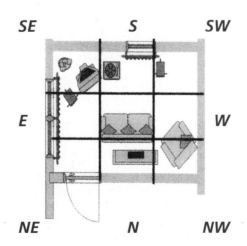

Energize the south with lights, the brighter the better. Chandeliers are the best lights to look for. Also anything red ...

Energize the southwest and northeast with crystals. These are the earth element corners.

Energize the west and northwest with wind chimes, bells and anything metallic. These are the metal corners. Placing the television and stereo system in this corner also activates metal.

bad shar. It is better to have the coffee table in the centre and the sofas placed around it.

Activating good luck

There are several feng shui methods of activating good luck in the living room. In this book I would like to share with you two effective techniques; the first method has to do with the five elements of the eight directions, while the second method uses the four precious gems that bring good fortune.

Energizing with elements is the more commonly known of the two methods. This involves identifying the ruling element of each side or corner of the living room, and then activating that element by placing an object that strongly symbolizes that element. To use this method, superimpose the nine-sector grid over the room and from there identify the corners and the relevant elements. Then energize with any of the list of objects suggested with the illustration at the foot of page 107. Don't feel impelled to use every single object listed, however; in feng shui it is not necessary to overdo things. You will find that less is sometimes better than more.

Energizing with the four precious gems of good fortune

This method involves identifying these precious gems. It is based on the symbolic references to the four treasures that are identified as being associated with each of the four main directions.

In the south: hang lanterns to bring honour and a good name to the family.

In the west: bury five lucky coins to create wealth for the descendants.

In the east: grow a bamboo plant to enjoy good health and a long life.

In the north: place a lotus plant in a bowl of water to have an illustrious career.

Choosing furniture

New furniture is preferable to antiques. Unless you are completely knowl-edgeable about the provenance of old furniture, it is not a good idea to bring old furniture into your home as it could be imbued with a great deal of bad or tragic energy. Feng shui is a practice that attempts to create and accumulate good energy. Antique furniture usually have stale energy cling-ing to them, and this old energy may not blend harmoniously with your other furniture. Worse, certain types of old furniture could well have harmful energies attached to them. Antique beds, and opium couches especially, should be viewed with some suspicion.

If you want a cabinet or two for your living room bear in mind that there are many different styles of cabinets, ranging from the very elaborate-ly styled art nouveau type designs fashioned out of maples and walnuts to the heavy Oriental cabinets made from dark-wood or rosewood. Whatever style you choose, make sure they never seem sinister, and sharp edges should be rounded and made less threatening.

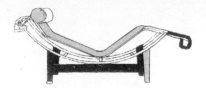

High-backed sofa sets that offer good back and side support are excellent from a feng shui viewpoint. These are much more comfortable and definitely more auspicious than the low backed sofas and armchairs.

This award-winning easy chair lacks the two arm rests. But because it has a steel frame, it is excellent for the northwest and west corners of a room.

Low-backed sofas lack support.

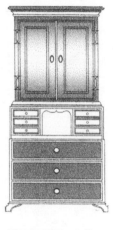

Above: Place tall cabinets such as this against a solid wall.

Below: The cross designs featured in this cabinet create discord and are not recommended. Cross symbols inside a home create shar chi.

Avoid those cabinets that are heavily carved and decorated with fierce animals. The energy of such heavy pieces will overwhelm a small home. Better to stick to furniture with simple lines. Cabinets that feature crosses, diamonds and any kind of pointed designs, do not have any good luck to offer their owners. The cabinet illustrated below left, for example, would be an excellent piece of furniture if it were not for the decorative pattern of criss-crossing lines on its front.

When shopping for furniture, develop awareness for what could hurt your feng shui unnecessarily. A good rule of thumb is that any piece of furniture, which does not have threatening edges, is good. Also, any furniture that allows you to hide your daily clutter is good. So do go for furniture that comes with doors rather than exposed shelves. Bookshelves that do not have doors represent a threat to your general well-being. The result of being subject to open bookshelves is that you will not end your career in a good way. There will be problems when your astrological good luck runs out.

Placing and arranging furniture

When placing and arranging your furniture throughout the home, never block the flow of chi. Tall cabinets, tables or chairs should not overwhelm entrances into rooms nor confront main doors, and the sharp edges of tables should never point at entrances or sitting areas since that would be tantamount to sending disturbing and harmful chi outwards.

Custom-made furniture built to blend harmoniously with the living space creates good feng shui. With this type of furniture, the danger of poison arrows is reduced because

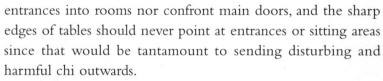

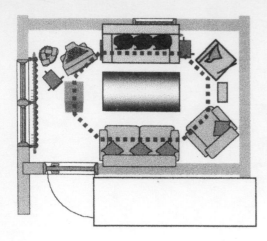

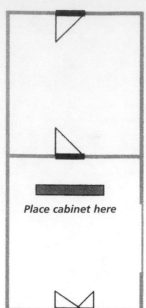

Left: A lucky sofa arrangement stimulates the Pa Kua.

Right: A tall cabinet like the one featured on page 109 is excellent for correcting three doors in a straight line when placed in front of the second door as shown.

Place cabinet here

built-in furniture is usually designed to be flush with walls, and to fit nicely into corners.

Arrange sofas to form a regular shape: rectangular or square, or the best arrangement is in the shape of a Pa Kua, the eight-sided octagonal shape that is considered extremely auspicious both for living room furniture and when used as dining table tops. Arrange sofas so that they surround a coffee table and then place small side tables between the sofas to simulate the diagonal sides of the Pa Kua. This arrangement creates much social and networking luck for the family, and it is conducive to fostering goodwill and good relationships within the family. It is also regarded as a complete arrangement with nothing missing.

Living room sofa sets can have square or rectangular coffee tables in the centre which symbolize the earth and wood elements respectively. Both of these elements are auspicious for the living room. Avoid sofa arrangements that create an L- or a U-shape since these suggest something incomplete or missing.

Place tall cabinets against a solid wall, unless they are being specifically used to create a room divider, or used as a feng shui tool. For instance, tall cabinets make excellent and effective blocks when there are, say, three doors in a straight line. Otherwise, they should not appear to float in any room with no back support. If they are fitted with mirrors, check to see what these mirrors are reflecting. The big taboos are if the mirrors reflect toilets, the main door, or the staircase. If they reflect food or a pleasant garden, caught through a picture window, the effect is harmless.

Doubling wealth in the dining room

The dining room should be located at, or very near, the centre of the home, or at least in the middle portion of the home. Ideally, it should be laid out between the living room and the kitchen. This central location blends agreeably with the centre being the heart of the home, thereby creating the luck of family unity. There is greater likelihood of harmony between the parents and between siblings. Like the living room, dining areas should be regular in shape. All protruding or oddly-shaped corners should be camouflaged either with plants or decorative furniture. Tall cabinets and Korean chests would be ideal.

Common feng shui problems connected with dining rooms usually have to do with their placement in relation to the overall layout of the home. Because the dining room represents the heart of the home where the family gathers, this is a room that should be kept yang and be filled with yang energy through music, happy colours and brightly painted or papered walls. It is also very important to counter any room and furniture arrangements that create an excess of yin energy since this can lead to serious bad luck. Here are some arrangements to avoid or counter.

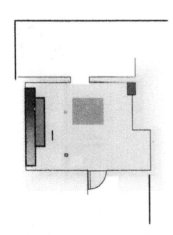

Above and right: The position of the dining room is important: try to place it as near to the centre of the house as possible as this room represents the heart of the home. The worst positioning for a dining room would be beneath a toilet.

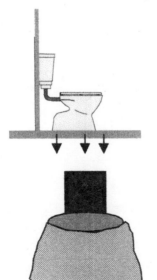

◆The most important taboos have to do with the dining table being inadvertently placed directly beneath a toilet on an upper floor. Eating under a kitchen stove or a washing machine is also bad, but not as harmful. If you live beneath someone else's apartment, familiarize yourself with the layout above.

You can then make sure that you do not place important pieces of furniture under unlucky objects on upper floors. Remember that it is not only toilets that cause damage. In addition, kitchen stoves, ovens, washing machines, and heavy furniture like pianos can also be harmful if positioned above the dining room.

◆ Rooms with windows on two opposite walls should not be used as the dining area. This causes chi to charge inauspiciously across the dining table, thereby upsetting the family's rice bowls.

◆ Rooms with one wall shared with a toilet should not be used as a dining area. If you do, make sure side tables where food is served are not placed against such a wall.

◆ The dining room should not have a full view of, or be too near to the main front door. If it is, then placing a screen between the door and the dining table softens the negative effect of this feature.

◆ Ancestral portraits should not be placed in the dining room. These pictures of dead family members are much too yin to be placed in this area. Far better to hang them in the living room or in the foyer of the home. They are also not suitable in the bedrooms.

◆ This part of the house should not be excessively yang either. If a window or door opens to the glare of the afternoon sun, install shades to nullify the effect of too much sun.

◆ Do refrain from displaying antique furniture and antique statues in the dining room. They are too yin. I once ate at a Chinese restaurant that had been strangely named the Museum, and in keeping with its theme, the decorative items on display were all artefacts and antique statues that sent out huge amounts of tiresome yin energy. It was one of the worst meals of my life and I have not been back. Needless to say, the restaurant did extremely badly. If you have antique furniture, put it in the living room. If possible, refrain from buying antique furniture and statues altogether. They are not good feng shui, and are more suitable in a museum.

Antique or other Buddha statues should not be in the dining room. Place them near the foyer or in the living room instead.

Doubling family wealth

The best method for symbolically doubling the family wealth is to place a full size mirror on one wall of the dining room. Then, when the mirror reflects the food on the dining table it is said to be most auspicious. And should you also decide to add a sideboard next to the mirror and place on it the three Star Gods – Fuk Luk Sau (see pages 66-7) – the symbolism of prosperity is complete.

◆ It is vital that the dining room be free of exposed overhead beams since sitting and eating under such heaviness creates recurring health problems. If you already have beams in your dining room, either try to camouflage them with a false ceiling as described on page 97 or arrange the dining table so that no one sits directly beneath any of the beams. Nor should ceilings have any elaborate designs as they could inadvertently cause feng shui problems by sending shar chi onto the food consumed by the family.

◆ Sunken dining rooms are not a good idea, either. Dining rooms must always be higher in floor level than living rooms. In homes that have split floor levels on the ground floor, this becomes an important factor in the layout arrangement of rooms. Should the dining area be sunken, powerful up-lights placed on the floor should help to raise the chi, as should tall plants placed at the corners of the dining rooms. In fact, placing plants in the dining area is always a good idea since plants represent growth.

Different shapes for dining tables

Dining tables should be round, oval or square in shape although the round shape is said to be superior. This is because the round shape represents the metal element and, in this case, it symbolizes gold, signifying prosperity for the residents. Round dining tables also signify a never-ending unity and presence for the family. The symbolism is thus most auspicious.

Do not have a table that seats four people since four is considered an inauspicious number. Six or eight will be fine since both of these numbers are deemed auspicious. Try to place each member of the family in the seat that allows them to tap their individual auspicious directions according to the tables on pages 75-6. Sitting down to dine while facing your best direction ensures good feng shui while eating.

Dining tables in the East
I like my dining table to be made of either rosewood or with a marble top, and those that come with elaborate mother of pearl insets are most auspicious. I am, of course, referring to traditional Chinese dining tables. Those of you who have been invited into traditional wealthy Chinese homes, whether in Hong Kong, Singapore, Taiwan or Malaysia, will find that the dining table in these families is always round, have a single solid stand in the centre, and almost always have the most elaborate dragon carvings or pearl inlaid decorative motifs. This is the height of auspicious dining and it brings excellent feng shui.

Food in the dining room

Paintings in the dining room should have auspicious fruits or food as the subject. It is very auspicious to have fruits in a still-life since this symbolizes a good life with plenty to eat. Paintings of the peach symbolize longevity, while oranges and pineapples mean a 'welcome to wealth!' Good fortune fruits either represented in paintings or fashioned out of crystal, cloisonné or jade, make excellent decorative subjects for the dining room.

Remember that to the Chinese, the symbolism of eating and food is synonymous with prosperity. Chinese greet each other with the words, 'Have you eaten?' The Chinese are also very conscious of material wealth. During the lunar New Year, people celebrate by sending auspicious gifts to each other, and when they meet, they wish each other Kung Hei Fatt Choy, which translated means 'Congratulations, may your luck expand'.

Food on the table is therefore a most auspicious feature and if this can be enhanced by hanging a mirror on the wall, so much the better as this is said to double your wealth. Do not, however, confuse the dining room with the kitchen. Mirrors placed in the kitchen, especially when reflecting the stove, are most harmful. The act of cooking food over the fire is totally different from the act of eating. One denotes the servant preparing the food while the other denotes the master eating the feast. Do recall that feng shui is symbolic. This is fundamental to interpreting feng shui recommendations.

Above: Never sit facing the sharp edge of a table. Round tables are better.

Below: To have fruits or food in a painting in the dining room is auspicious.

Sleeping for success in the bedrooms

The feng shui of the master bedroom exerts great influence over the marital happiness of the couple. When the chi of the bedroom is harmonious and conducive to good fortune, the couple will enjoy a supportive and successful relationship. Each will fulfil their appropriate role within the family. Health does not suffer, misunderstandings are kept to a minimum, and there will definitely be no separation and no divorce.

When the chi in the bedroom is not harmonious, over time there develops a great bitterness between the couple. There is no success and no support in the relationship, and certainly no conjugal happiness. There will most likely be third party intervention in the marriage leading to quarrels and recriminations. Communication grinds to a halt. There will simply be so much unhappiness.

If you are one half of a couple, then, it is worth investing in good bedroom feng shui since so much of your life rests on the relationship with your loved one. But sleeping for success does not just refer to happiness between a couple. The meaning of success should be seen in the widest meaning of the word, for if your sleeping direction and orientation enjoys excellent feng shui, then the good fortune is manifested in all dimensions of your life. You will enjoy success at work and in your outside relationships; you will have good health, and you will definitely have a happy home and family life. So how do you go about ensuring good feng shui in the bedroom?

First, make sure you have a regular shape. The best shapes are square or rectangular. If you have an attached bathroom, keep it quite separate, and let it not create an L-shaped bedroom. The toilet of an L-shaped bedroom creates several inter-related problems. The two most damaging are the creation of a missing corner, and the placement of the toilet in one corner of the room, which may correspond to the occupant's good direction. This would result in the good luck being pressed down. The corner also creates a poison arrow that is aimed at the bed, as illustrated overleaf (top). The

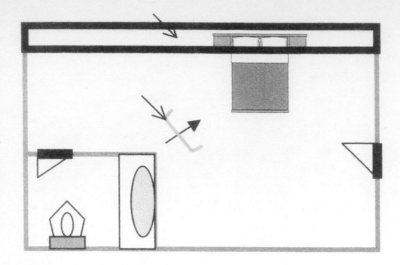

An inauspiciously laid out bedroom. The position of the bathroom has created a missing corner, an irregular shape, and a corner with a poison arrow. For better feng shui in this room, the occupant needs to bring in a screen to block off the poison arrows and hang bamboo rods tied with red ribbon on the protruding beam above the bed.

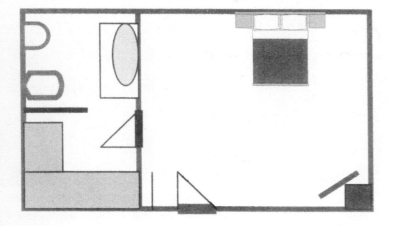

An auspiciously laid out bedroom. The bedroom shape has remained regular with no missing corners. Corners that protrude send shar chi, but this problem has been corrected with a cabinet.

illustration also shows how a protruding beam above the headboard sends shar chi to anyone sleeping below.

Any one or all of the harmful features mentioned can cause severe bad luck for the occupants of a bedroom. Deflect the bad energy of an overhead beam by placing bamboo stems tied with red thread (see page 63) along the edges of the beam. Place a decorative screen to block off the poison arrow of the corner. The screen can either be placed as shown in the illustration, or it can be used to regularize the shape of the bedroom, and transform it into a more manageable rectangle.

A good layout arrangement for master bedrooms with attached bathrooms is to have the two rooms next to each other. The layout of the two rooms, however, must be such that the doors are not placed in a straight line, nor hit at the bed. Nor should the bed and toilet share a wall. Look at the layout in the illustration above (bottom). Here the toilet has been designed to be far away from where the bed is placed in the bedroom and the protruding corner has been camouflaged with a cabinet. This type of softening is preferable to plants, since plants and water features should never be placed in the bedroom.

The bedroom door

The position of the door into the bedroom can often cause problems and some of the more common are listed here. Please note that one possible option facing you is to re-locate the door, but this is not always possible. Together with each of the taboos is a suggested way to correct, or at least to diminish the problem:

1 The bedroom door should never be positioned in a straight line with the door into a toilet or bathroom. This causes severe bad luck, especially if the bed then lies between the two doors. In such a situation, you are strongly advised to place a screen or divider just in front of the bathroom door. The screen divider should shut out the view of the door from the bed altogether.

2 The door of the bedroom should not directly face a staircase on the outside. If the staircase is too near, the chi will become very fierce and it would be absolutely necessary to install a very bright light on the ceiling between the staircase and the door.

3 The door of the bedroom should not directly face another door across a corridor or landing. This is a confrontational mode that creates quarrels and misunderstandings. Instead, hang a beaded curtain to soften the effect of confronting doors. The situation is worse if it faces a half door, ie if the two doors are not aligned to each other. In such a situation, try to place something between the two doors. It can be a plant or any kind of divider.

4 The bedroom should not open out to a corner cased by two walls at ninety degrees to each other. If the bedroom is situated like this, then place a creeper plant against the edge to diffuse the killing breath being sent towards the door.

Major taboos in the bedroom

Never forget that the bedroom is a place of rest and relaxation. The energies that prevail in the bedroom should be more yin than yang since a bedroom that is too yang will cause its residents to be overly active. In view of this it is easy to understand why feng shui experts and masters strenuously warn against activating the bedroom with too many good fortune symbols.

Water

Hence, although water is said to bring wealth, and water features are generally auspicious, it is a grave mistake to place water features in the bedroom. If you sleep, for example, with an aquarium behind you, you will either get robbed, burgled or suffer a financial loss. Leave the water features in the living room and in the garden. Water in this case refers not merely to fishbowls and fountains but also and especially to paintings which have a view of the sea or a scenic lake, or a waterfall. Keep such paintings well away from your bed. The colour blue, however, is acceptable for the bedroom, even though it represents water, but avoid the colour black.

Flowers and plants

It sounds awful, I know, but it is not a good idea to display flowers and plants in the bedroom, especially growing plants. These are symbols of extremely strong yang energy. Placed in a woman's bedroom, the plants spoil all romance luck. Placed in a couple's bedroom, the flowers cause quarrels and infidelity. Paintings that have flowers as subjects are also not encouraged. The only time when flowers are said to bring good luck is when you want to bring active yang energy into the room and this happens when someone is recuperating from an illness. Even then it is not good to keep the flowers in the room for too long.

Do not display flowers in the bedroom; they spoil your romance luck.

Mirrors

Having a mirror facing the bed is a major taboo. If anything could wreck a marriage, a mirror in the bedroom could. I have always strongly advised against having large mirrors that face the bed, whether they are placed on a wall, on the ceiling or on the doors of cupboards. Mirrors reflect the sleeping couple, sending shar chi their way, causing misunderstandings, and often causing the partners to become unfaithful to each other. Mirrors in the bedroom also bring the entrée of a third party into a marriage. In fact, anything that has a reflective surface should be kept outside the bedroom. If you have a television, do place a cloth over it to cover the screen before you go to bed. If you have mirrors facing your bed, dismantle or cover them with a curtain. Do not spoil your marriage with mirrors.

Inauspicious bed positions

Don't place your bed:
1 under a beam.
2 facing a door: either the bedroom or the toilet.
3 between two doors.
4 so it shares a wall with a toilet.
5 under a window.
6 opposite a protruding corner.
7 facing a mirror.
8 directly under a water storage tank.

The direction on this bed shows how positions are calculated for orientating a bed. It is the direction in which your head is pointing that counts.

Open shelves

If you have open bookshelves that directly face the bed, it is only a matter of time before you get sick. Open shelves symbolize blades cutting into you as you sleep. In fact, open shelves are not good feng shui anywhere. I strongly urge you to have doors fixed to these shelves unless you have books placed in the shelves in a way that nullifies the blade effect.

Sleeping directions

To start with, your bed should not be encumbered, blocked or being hurt by poison arrows that bring illness and bad luck. Having taken care that nothing in your personal environment is hurting you while you sleep, the next step in feng shui is to consciously tap your auspicious sleeping directions.

Feng shui prescribes specific auspicious sleeping directions that are based on the Pa Kua Lo Shu formula (see pages 72-4). Once you know your Kua number you can then ascertain your auspicious and inauspicious directions depending on whether you are an east or west group person (see pages 75-6). The way to use these directions is to select the kind of luck you want to activate, and then orientate your bed in such a way that you sleep with your head pointed towards the desired direction (the direction of the arrow in the illustration above is the direction).

The four excellent directions of your group offer four different types of good luck. The first type is the best since it brings the luck of success in all your endeavours. This direction is also called the sheng chi direction. Those in business or a career and wanting more wealth should sleep with their heads pointing to this direction.

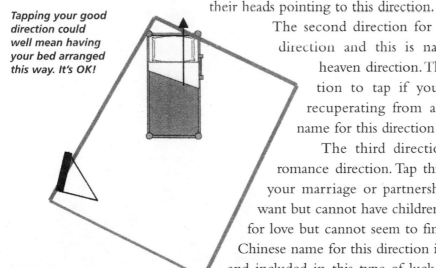

Tapping your good direction could well mean having your bed arranged this way. It's OK!

The second direction for sleeping is your health direction and this is named the doctor from heaven direction. This is an excellent direction to tap if you are not well, or are recuperating from an illness. The Chinese name for this direction is tien yi.

The third direction is your family and romance direction. Tap this direction if you want your marriage or partnership to be sound, if you want but cannot have children, and if you are looking for love but cannot seem to find the right person. The Chinese name for this direction is the nien yen direction and included in this type of luck are romance, marriage,

The Yang Dwelling Classic

According to this popular classic, there are several methods of determining the bedrooms for different members of the family.

1 Elderly people should sleep in bedrooms that have a west orientation. In the Forbidden City in Beijing, all the palaces set aside for the older ladies of the court are on the west side of the City. This is because the energies of the west rooms are said to be more conducive to the older generation. This recommendation coincides with the Pa Kua method for allocating bedrooms since, according to the Pa Kua, the northwest should be the place of elderly patriarchs, while the southwest should be the place of elderly matriarchs.

2 Growing children, especially the young sons of the family, should sleep in the east where yang energies are at their zenith. Also according to the Pa Kua method, the east is identified as being the best place for the eldest son.

3 The eldest daughter should have her bedroom in the southeast. Both these directions are of the wood element, which represents exuberant growth.

fidelity, good children and togetherness as a family unit.

The fourth direction is called the fu wei direction and this brings the luck of self-development. Those still pursuing their studies or working towards a degree should sleep with their heads pointing in this direction.

The practical side of using these wonderful auspicious directions can sometimes be quite tricky. Sometimes, for example, you will find that tapping your so-called directions can turn out to be impossible. This is because most bedrooms are very small and cramped, and after satisfying all the taboos listed previously you might feel a sense of frustration that comes with not being able to use your directions.

Another frustration is that room orientations are almost never conveniently facing exactly one of the cardinal points. Compass directions in real life are never so clear cut, and you may find that you need to place your bed in an awkward place. And in doing so you may not even be sleeping in your first best direction! Perhaps the orientation of your room allows you only to tap your second best direction.

Improving your love life with feng shui

Romance and love luck can also be improved by ensuring that the love corner – the southwest – of your bedroom is further energized with the placement of auspicious objects that symbolize marital bliss. The best symbols for a great love life are the displaying of a pair of mandarin ducks. Don't keep one or three, keep a pair. If you keep one duck it means nothing and if you keep three you will only become a flirt. Get those wooden carved ducks from a Chinese supermarket. If ducks are hard to find, you can substitute with a pair of lovebirds – budgerigars.

Another wonderful symbol is the double happiness sign which is the universal Chinese symbol for a happy marriage. You can also place a picture of a heart in the southwest. A more sophisticated method involves the use of lights. Crystal lights are the most effective. Hang a small crystal chandelier in this part of your bedroom and keep the light on for at least three hours each night.

Keeping romance alive in the bedroom

Frequently marriages fail because the feng shui of the bedroom is all wrong. It is not possible to enumerate all and everything that could possibly go wrong, but major problems include the following.

- Never have a large mirror directly facing or above the bed.
- A television screen in the bedroom leads to separation of the couple.
- Do not sleep with a large overhead beam cutting the bed into two. The horrible energy coming from above symbolically divides the bed into two, and so splits the couple in the same way.
- Don't have a toilet above you. Never sleep in a bedroom that is located directly below a toilet on the upper floor. The toilet shoots unhappy chi down from above, causing problems between the couple.
- Don't sleep on a double bed with two single mattresses. This creates a symbolic separation that could well become real. If each member of a couple has a different set of auspicious directions, it is far better to have two single beds, and even two different bedrooms. But sleeping on the same double bed, which has two separate mattresses, is bad.
- Check your own personal romance direction based on your Kua number (see page 119) and arrange your sleeping direction to tap into your personal romance direction.

Much of feng shui is compromise. Out of the four directions there will be at least one good direction you can use. Remember that sleeping with your head orientated towards one of your good directions at least means that you will not then be sleeping in a harmful direction.

The other four inauspicious directions are very harmful, and my advice has always been to go for any one of the four good directions, no matter how difficult it is to do so.

If a couple sharing a bed have different sets of auspicious directions, feng shui always prescribes that it is the man, or patriarch, whose auspicious direction should prevail. But if you are a woman and you are sleeping in a double bed with your partner and you are the one having problems, then irrespective of his personal nien yen direction, and even if it is different from yours, you should move your bed to benefit your direction.

There is no easy way to accommodate two sets of lucky directions in a partnership. When both persons have the same set of directions, feng shui is easy to practice. When each has a different direction, there are some tough decisions to be made.

Good fortune symbols in the bedroom

You can energize good fortune if you place symbolic good luck objects under the bed. These good luck objects will depend on what kind of luck you want.

- ◆ For extra protection or to attract good opportunities, place a double fish symbol, either as a drawing or in gold, under the mattress on the side where your head is.

- ◆ If you wish to generate lots of travel luck, place a conch shell under your mattress. The shell is also excellent for those in the communication business. Actually, any kind of

decorative shell is acceptable although something that looks like the shell in the illustration to the below is supposed to be particularly lucky.

- ◆ If you want your marriage to be smooth, place the double happiness symbol under the bed. It also helps childless couples who may be having a hard time conceiving.

- ◆ To attract good energy during the hours of sleep, place a mystic knot tied with red under the mattress. This symbol represents a never-ending cycle of good fortune.

Bedroom furniture

The main piece of furniture in the bedroom is the bed and the way this bed is constructed, its headboard, and the kinds of mattress you use, have feng shui connotations.

Never sleep on round beds and waterbeds. I can think of nothing worse than sleeping on something so apparently unstable. In fact, the best criteria for judging how auspicious a bed is to see how stable and sturdy it is. Never sleep on an unstable bed so make sure it is fixed firmly in place.

The headboard of a bed also has feng shui meanings although my experience has shown that this is not significant. The only things I would advise are that beds should definitely have headboards and that they should be solid rather than hollow. If the headboard is missing, the indications are that the bed is not auspicious. Brass headboards are not encouraged, and semi-circular headboards are not as auspicious as rectangular ones since a semi-circle suggests that something is missing.

Feng shui in the kitchen

In feng shui lore, the kitchen is traditionally the part of the home that is supposed to be the most unlucky. If you use the Kua formula to determine your good and bad directions you will know what your total loss direction is, and this is supposedly the best location for the kitchen. Why ? Because the daily use of the stove ignites the fire, which in turn creates the energy to successfully press down on the bad luck.

The kitchen is also the place where the two opposing elements of water and fire interact, and feng shui in the kitchen involves the correct balancing of these two elements. An auspicious interaction will bring enormous good luck, while a faulty one will lead to adverse consequences. What is good or bad interaction is determined by the position of the stove in relation to the position of the sink.

To balance water and fire in the kitchen, do not position the oven or stove directly opposite the sink or refrigerator. Doing this puts the two elements in a confrontational mode. Nor should you position the two elements too close to each other. To ensure this does not happen, put a cabinet or kitchen cupboard between the refrigerator or sink and stove.

Cooking food

In addition, the way the food is cooked also affects the family's luck. In fact, more so. This is expressed in terms of stove orientation. In the old days, feng shui guidelines on stove orientation would be easy to follow since this is expressed in terms of the direction of the oven mouth. The cooking stove of the old days was a simple implement. The mouth was the opening in front of the stove where wood or charcoal was set ablaze. In this way, it was easy to know how to orientate the oven mouth according to the most auspicious direction.

Above: The oven mouth.

Right: Where the arrow is pointing is where the good energy should be coming from.

Modern kitchens no longer use stoves like that, and it is difficult trying to determine the mouth of the oven, or the cooker. When I went back to the source books for assistance, I discovered that the rationale for using the oven mouth was that, for the food being cooked to be auspicious, the energy fuelling the fire had to come from the

Other guidelines on stove placement

Do not put the stove or oven:

◆ directly in front of the door that comes into the kitchen. This is a dangerous arrangement especially if the kitchen is too near the front door.

◆ facing a toilet. If it does, please keep the toilet door closed whenever any cooking is being done.

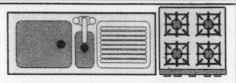

Above: Water should not be placed next to fire. So the sink should not be next to the stove. Nor should they be directly opposite each other.

◆ in front of a window. Contrary to conventional wisdom, a window above a stove denotes a sorry lack of support.

Above: The stove should not be placed below a window.

◆ immediately under an exposed overhead beam or face a protruding corner.

◆ between two water features ie with the sink on one side and the refrigerator on the other side. This configuration will cause the family to be in mourning. It is said that fire between water denotes the shedding of tears.

◆ in a corner. If the stove is placed in a corner the cook will have to work facing a corner. the situation is dangerous.

◆ in the heart of the home. Kitchens should always be located in the inner half of the home, but never in the centre of a home.

◆ facing a staircase.

◆ directly under a toilet on the upper floor. If this is your problem move the stove and rearrange the layout of the kitchen.

◆ directly beneath a water tank on the roof. This puts out the fire - literally and creates amazingly bad luck.

◆ in the northwest sector of the kitchen as this is a dangerous location referred to as fire at heaven's gate.

best direction. Using this explanation as a guide, we have now determined that for electrical cooking implements the direction that the plug that goes into the kettle or cooker, say, is the important direction to take into consideration. For gas cookers, the oven mouth is where the gas actually enters the cooker.

For Chinese families it is a simple enough matter to use the rice cooker as symbolizing the main stove. Orientate this correctly and good feng shui is assured. In addition, I also orientate the kettle in an auspicious direction to obtain a double benefit. In this way, I ensure that the food and water served in our home are harmonious and auspicious. And because my family has both east and west group members, I use two rice cookers. This is the only way to handle the fact that the two halves of a couple could well belong to different groups, east and west.

Food areas

A refrigerator that is always well stocked brings excellent feng shui.

Good feng shui in the kitchen means having a well-stocked refrigerator at all times. This is the modern equivalent of the full rice urn. The Chinese go to great lengths to ensure that the rice urn is never empty. There should be rice in the urn at all times, and beneath the rice, they place a red packet stuffed with coins. This red packet which is supposed to be an auspicious continuation of good fortune from year to year, is replaced with a new one on the first day of each lunar new year. This practice has become a superstitious cultural practice among the people of Chinese origins and I didn't understand its real significance when I first saw my grandmother doing it. However, I have now been following this tradition for well over thirty years. This ensures that financially I will always have enough to eat.

Breakfast tables in the kitchen create a central focal point of interest that represents good feng shui. Such tables also serve the purpose of creating a barrier between sinks, refrigerators and washing machines on one side of the kitchen, and ovens and stoves on the other. This reduces the water-fire confrontation and brings harmony to the kitchen.

Onions, garlic and other dried preservatives hanging from the ceiling in the centre of the kitchen are not especially auspicious features. Nor are pots and pans hanging down from the centre of the kitchen.

PART **3**

Feng shui in your work and career

Feng shui and business

It is no longer a secret that many of the most wealthy and successful Chinese businessmen and women practice feng shui. For many of them, the mythical dragon of feng shui cosmology reigns, exerting enormous sway on office arrangements, on building design, on entrance orientations, on furniture placements, and on the timing of business and commercial decisions. In the world of Asian commerce, feng shui extends to those who covet it, a competitive edge. Those in business who use this ancient science believe they are adding an essential, if metaphysical, dimension to the modern day management of their businesses.

The expense of a reliable feng shui consultation for the businessman can sometimes seem prohibitive. Charges are often calculated according to square footage and rank of the manager or director asking for the feng shui reading. In spite of this, the feng shui expert, especially if he has a good reputation, is always consulted.

In Hong Kong, feng shui has received an official plug from no less a personage than the new Governor of this bustling metropolis. Tung Chee Hwa openly acknowledged that he believed strongly in feng shui. The shipping tycoon disdained inheriting the British Governor's office and home, dismissing both as having inauspicious feng shui, and then proceeded to select his own premises according to his own feng shui man's advice.

For years, of course, the business community of Hong Kong has accorded an important place to feng shui in their business decisions. Even expatriate, British managed firms retain feng shui men on their payroll. The most commonly quoted example of high profile feng shui at work is the Hong Kong Bank, whose impressive new head office building, built in the mid-eighties in central Hong Kong, carries a great deal of the feng shui man's inputs. Those in the know will swear that the bank's consistently impressive growth rates and profit records year after year are due, in part, to the good feng shui of their head office building. Those who dismiss feng shui as superstition could well view this as a debatable point. Nevertheless, the lineage of Taipans (the heads) of this august bank has given credence to feng shui advice for decades. Wisely they seem to have adopted the philosophy that since the bulk of their customers believe in feng shui, why not go with the flow? Practising feng shui is, after all, a no-loss situation, requiring nothing other than a relatively insignificant expense. Looking at how the bank has grown and prospered over the years, they seem to have done very well indeed.

Other less high profile users of feng shui have been the British retailing giant, Marks and Spencer, and almost all the hongs – or trading houses – of Hong Kong such as Jardines and Swires. It is also a widely acknowledged fact that most of the more successful of the colony's property developers, from Li Kar Shing to Lee Shau Kee to the Kwoks of Sun Hung Kai and the Chengs of the New World Group use feng shui as a matter of course. To them, feng shui is part and parcel of their heritage, their Chinese tradition and culture, and it features as an integral dimension of their business lives.

It is not just the rich and powerful who believe in feng shui. Its practice among the Chinese cuts across social class. For the practitioner of feng shui is tycoon and taxi driver, successful wealthy magnate and struggling, poor merchant. Feng shui cuts across the class and income spectrum, holding out the promise of continued prosperity for those who have made it, and of hitting the jackpot for those who have not.

What, then, are some of the more important feng shui tips for doing business? In addition to the basic essentials already dealt with, this section of the book looks at some of the techniques employed by the Chinese Taipans of the Far East.

Feng shui in other countries

It is the same story in Singapore and Malaysia. Here, businessmen, career people, corporate managers and small-time entrepreneurs of Chinese (and even other racial) origin can be found, who include feng shui features in the designs and layout plans of their homes and offices. In these two prosperous ASEAN nations, indications of feng shui inputs into real estate and housing projects are evident everywhere.

Likewise, in recent years, as news of the potency and good results of feng shui has spread, business people in the other countries, in Jakarta and Manila, especially among those of Chinese origin, have also turned to feng shui to provide additional insurance of success to their businesses.

Meanwhile, in faraway places like Australia, Britain and Europe, and in many American cities where feng shui is gaining wider acceptance, feng shui has yet to make it big in the boardrooms of corporations.

But because feng shui works, and because it can be learnt relatively easily, it is only a matter of time before it becomes equally popular among the business peoples of the West. Especially since in recent years, feng shui expertise has become increasingly accessible through the availability of simplified texts in the English language.

Auspicious and inauspicious buildings

In assessing the feng shui of any building, consider first the surrounding and approach roads that lead to it; and check to see if it blends in with the surrounding environment. Then look out for structures in the immediate environment which could have an effect, good or bad, on your building. Just as with the position of your home, neighbouring buildings that are taller and more imposing than yours can either be supporting of (good) or confronting (bad) your building. These are the external feng shui parameters that must always be investigated first, and the feng shui of a building is said to be auspicious if the factors outlined here are considered and taken care of.

Shapes of buildings that are unlucky

Being the only tall building is not auspicious, and being in the shadow of other more massive buildings is also not good. In the modern city landscape, tall high rises are like the mountains and hills of the natural environment. The overall effect should be one of undulating levels to simulate the auspicious green dragon.

When a single tower soars above all the rest, surrounding buildings that have their entrances directly facing it will suffer severely bad feng shui. If the tower is behind your building, it transforms into a benevolent protector and symbolically becomes the black turtle.

When there are two tall towers, they signify giant joss sticks, especially if the top of these tower blocks are lighted at night. The symbolism here is negative, and the city could well suffer from severely hostile breath emanating from the

Above: This is an excellent shape for a building.

Below: A taller tower standing behind your building is benevolent and will do you no

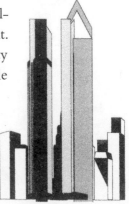

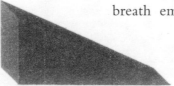

Some unlucky shapes for buildings (see also page 35)

Some common auspicious shapes viewed from the ground

Shapes of buildings in the city should be assessed from two dimensions ie the shape of the layout when seen from the air, and the shape when seen from ground level. From both these perspectives, the auspicious shapes are, as ever, the regular shapes – especially if they are rectangular. Undertake a simple element analysis of shapes of buildings to make your assessment.

The following shapes are commonly found in office blocks and only become inauspicious when there are missing corners.

Square shaped buildings are favourable, solid and strong. They belong to the earth element and would benefit almost everyone. Rectangular shaped buildings are more auspicious when soaring upwards, they belong to the wood element. When such buildings are also deep, the feng shui is considered excellent not just for the present but also the future.

Trapezoidal shapes on façades are better when the base is broader than the top. When in layout mode, it is considered more auspicious if the front is wider than the back. See also page 34.

tower blocks. If your office building is located near such tower blocks, once again having them behind you is better than in front of you.

Potential city hazards

The examples shown overleaf are common sights in the city. The presence of construction cranes, for instance, is increasing in the booming cities of the Far East. When these are compounded by excessive building activity, the feng shui of many buildings can be adversely affected until the cranes are actually removed. The tower shown overleaf (bottom right) represents very dangerous feng shui for any building that faces it.

In a city, commercial or industrial environment, there are many different types of buildings and other physical structures that can cause damage to your feng shui. It is a good idea to be wary of what can hurt. Some examples are illustrated overleaf. Remember that these structures hurt most when the main entrance of your building faces them, and that these are only examples:

◆ If the entrance to your workplace faces a water tank like the one that is featured overleaf (bottom left), your workplace does not have good feng shui unless the view is blocked from sight with trees or if your entrance is reoriented.

If your building faces a factory like the one shown here, several things will hurt you and everyone working in your building very severely. First, the smoking chimneys will cause all to suffer financial loss. Second, the triangular roof angles will cause everyone in the building affected by it to suffer a multitude of problems.

A construction crane that will bring bad feng shui to surrounding buildings.

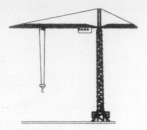

If the entrance to your workplace faces a water tank like this one, your workplace does not have good feng shui unless the view is blocked from sight with trees or if your entrance is re-orientated.

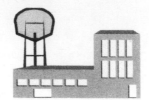

A tower such as this one creates very bad feng shui.

◆ A most harmful structure to watch out for is the presence of an arty sculpture which has sharp angles pointing in several directions. When something like this is positioned in front of corporate head office buildings and inadvertently sending hostile energies towards the building, the bad luck created can be quite severe. I have seen some desperately harmful (and ugly) sculptures in the City of London and also in New York City. If you work in a building afflicted by this unfortunate display of the owner's love of art, do not enter the building by the door that is hurt by the sculpture. Instead, you should look for another door to enter the building.

◆ Flyovers and overhead roads can be severely threatening. If you find that your building is unfortunate enough to be cut by high level or multi-level roads or overpasses, it is best for you and your company to plan on eventually moving out.

◆ The negative effect of elevated roads and railways is another feature of city feng shui. Those overhead light transit railways are bad news for apartment and office blocks unfortunate enough to be on the cutting outer edge of the railway track. When the railway line or elevated highway embraces a building, it brings protection luck, but if it cuts and slices into the belly of any building, then bad luck will have been created.

When the raised road wraps around a building, it does not hurt the building.

◆ You will find that just about the only way to overcome the cutting edge of a road is to dress the building in a veneer of mirror glass that reflects the road, thereby reflecting back its killing energy. Mirror panes can also be an effective cure for balancing parts of the building that are hit by other unsavoury structures that have been built nearby.

◆ Finally, there is one more location point to bear in mind. Usually, the faster the traffic flow is, the more dangerous the energy it creates. If your building lies next to a highway, for example, the traffic is probably travelling at great speed, causing the chi to rush past. The effect is most definitely inauspicious. But if your building is located in the heart of the city, where you find that traffic usually moves slowly, the effect of the road becomes auspicious instead.

Building entrances

The entrance of buildings should be auspiciously sited to attract good flows of sheng chi, and the best indication of the availability of this chi is when there is an empty plot of land directly fronting the building. A parade ground, a football field, a public park – any of these free spaces, referred to as the bright hall – represent excellent feng shui. This is where the energy that brings good luck can settle, accumulate, and then enter your building. Everyone working in such a building will benefit from the good fortune that such an entrance creates.

It is not difficult to differentiate lucky from unlucky buildings. Just look at the main entrance into the building and see what it faces. In addition to an empty piece of land, the presence of a water feature is also highly auspicious. The most ideal of these water features are fountains, fish ponds and moving water. You can be as creative as you wish, but as long as the water is within view of the building's entrance, and is flowing towards rather than away from the building, the water will be auspicious.

Facing this empty piece of land brings excellent feng shui to this building.

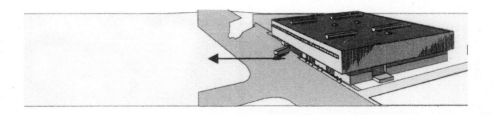

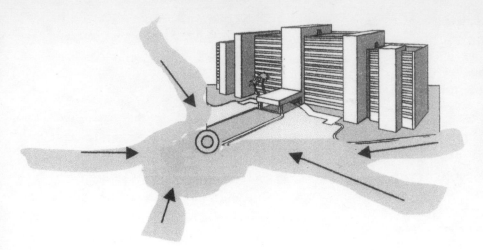

This building benefits from the five feeder roads bringing good chi towards the small patch of green where chi accumulates before entering the building. A small fountain built here would enhance the feng shui still further.

The best way to spot a building that has excellent feng shui, is to investigate the number of roads that appear to be feeding the front of the building. When there are several roads flowing towards the front and there is a water feature that encourages the auspicious chi brought by the roads to settle and accumulate, the feng shui of the building is greatly enhanced.

The building illustrated above benefits from the five feeder roads bringing good chi towards the small patch of green where chi accumulates before entering the building. A small fountain built here would enhance the feng shui still further.

If the building is also regular in shape and is not being attacked by hostile and other oddly shaped structures, you can work inside such a building and be assured that it will not cause you to suffer from bad luck.

Foyer areas

Foyer areas that welcome the chi should have auspicious features. For a

Auspicious water flows

If the water is flowing past the building, either in the form of an artificial waterway, a drain, a canal or a natural river, the direction of flow of this water will be extremely auspicious if the flow is in accordance with the water dragon formula, as outlined below. Please note that the direction of flow is taken standing at the main entrance looking out - not looking in.

◆ Water must flow from left to right past the main entrance if the main entrance faces a cardinal direction: north, south, east or west.

◆ Water must flow from right to left if the main entrance faces a secondary direction: northeast, northwest, southeast or southwest.

building to enjoy good feng shui there should be a distinct main lobby. I have seen many buildings that have more than one entrance and more than one main lobby and it seems like there are too many mouths. The energy of such buildings is sure to be unbalanced. Companies and occupants working inside buildings that have too many entrances, tend to quarrel and be unsettled. There can be no good luck.

Car parks should always be built underground, and never on the above ground, lower floors of the building. This creates empty space in the lower half of the building, symbolising a lack of foundation. In buildings where the offices are sitting on top of several levels of parking floors, and where the ground floor is kept empty so that the entire building seems like it is standing on stilts, the feng shui is exceptionally bad.

Other ways to ensure you have an auspicious foyer include ensuring the foyer is well lit, is spacious, and that it is properly decorated in accordance with the intrinsic energy of its location. Get the compass direction of the foyer location and decorate it to activate and strengthen the ruling element. If the foyer is located in the:

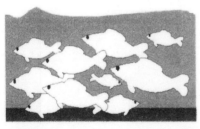

An aquarium containing a suitable number of fish (see right) in the foyer will enhance the office's luck.

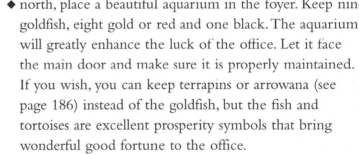

♦ north, place a beautiful aquarium in the foyer. Keep nine goldfish, eight gold or red and one black. The aquarium will greatly enhance the luck of the office. Let it face the main door and make sure it is properly maintained. If you wish, you can keep terrapins or arrowana (see page 186) instead of the goldfish, but the fish and tortoises are excellent prosperity symbols that bring wonderful good fortune to the office.

♦ south, southwest or northeast, place a beautiful crystal chandelier here. This feature will attract huge amounts of sheng chi into your office. There truly is nothing better than the chandelier for energizing and stimulating the flow of positive energy, but chandeliers are most potent when hung near the front door and in these three direction corners. Placed elsewhere they have less feng shui significance but they do not do any harm.

♦ southwest, northeast, west and northwest, simulate a brick wall design in your foyer. This will be such excellent feng shui and especially if the

Improving the chi energy in a foyer with three entrances

This illustration shows a building with three entrances, each of which is marked **A**. The foyer also suffers from a further harmful feature in that one of the entrances faces a bank of elevators (**B**). This is bad, as bad as facing an escalator, as this sort of layout causes chi to disintegrate very quickly. Meanwhile, another entrance faces a staircase descending to the basement car park (**C**). There are thus three main features that need to be corrected.

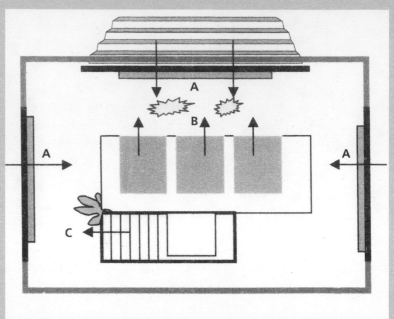

To overcome the problems, place bright lights between the elevators and the entrance; put green plants next to the staircase, and close at least one of the doors.

name of the company is then mounted on the wall in metallic colours or materials. This feature energizes the sheer power of the earth element. By adding the element of metal, you are creating a powerful and harmonious mix of good energy. Because all this is happening near the main door, the good fortune is magnified.

Successful office layouts

Good office layout can be vitally helpful for any company's overall financial fortunes. It also promotes good feelings among the staff, boosts productivity, and reduces friction, backbiting and politicking. Good office layout, with rooms and room usage arranged according to feng shui guidelines, also promotes a healthy environment where the incidences of illness are significantly reduced. Good office feng shui benefits every person who occupies the office ... but not equally.

There are always areas of the office that are more auspicious than others. Some rooms are more lucky than others. If you think about specific rooms in your office and start to trace the careers of former occupants, you will be able to identify certain rooms that seem to have brought luck to former occupants. Likewise, there will be rooms that have always brought ill luck. Occupants get sick, get the sack or suffer some personal tragedy. Be wary of such rooms.

At the same time, those whose office location, orientation and sitting direction blend harmoniously with their personal Kua numbers will benefit more from their sitting direction than those who do not use this formula feng shui to help them (see pages 72-6). Nevertheless, if your place at work has good feng shui, you will still enjoy good luck.

To benefit everybody, the whole office should be regular in shape. A perfect rectangle or square guarantees that every type of good luck is possible. When there is a missing corner in the office, the luck represented by the direction of the missing corner will be sorely lacking. The way to diagnose the compass location of a missing corner is to stand in the middle of the floor space with a reliable compass. Look for the direction north and then mark out the eight directions after you have superimposed a nine-sector grid onto the floor space. Ignore minor corners when you superimpose the grid. And make sure that each of the nine sectors created is more or less the same size. You should be as accurate as possible when using compass feng shui methods.

◆ If the north is missing, occupants find it tough to advance in their careers.
◆ If the south is missing, occupants have to put up with gossip, slander and a great deal of back biting and politicking.

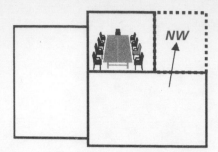

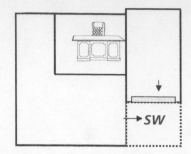

The missing corner in this office is the northwest which is bad news as there will be no support within the company for each other.

The missing corner in this office is the southwest which affects relationships within the office. Correct the problem with a wall mirror.

- If the west is missing, occupants could have family problems.
- If the east is missing, the health of occupants will suffer.
- If the northwest corner is missing, everyone in the office will suffer the bad luck of not getting any kind of support from the company or from the big boss. The northwest is the place that represents help from influential people. If this corner is missing, probably every occupant in the building will experience a lack of this luck. The way to overcome this problem is to artificially create the corner with a floor-length mirror (but see box, right).
- If the southwest corner is missing, the office will suffer from a great deal of bickering and human behaviour in your organization will leave a lot to be desired. This is the corner that brings the luck of good relationships and social interactions.
- If the northeast corner is missing, occupants find it hard to improve themselves.
- If the southeast of the floor space is missing, it affects the wealth luck. This is a very serious flaw in any office, and should be corrected if possible with a mirror, or by keeping the southeast wall very brightly lit. Placing lots of plants on this wall is also an excellent way of making up for the missing corner. When the east corner is missing, the luck that is affected is the health of the workers in the office. Use a mirror in the same way for dealing with this.

> ## Using mirrors in offices
> Many feng shui experts recommend the use of mirrors to correct missing corners. Personally, I feel that mirrors are more suitable for shops than for offices. But mirrors do the job of correcting missing corners very well. If you use mirrors, here are some basic rules:
> 1 Do not use mirror tiles, they are bad news, and cause more harm.
> 2 Make the mirror large enough to symbolically create an entire corner.
> 3 The mirror should be higher than the tallest person so no one's head gets cut off in the reflection, and it should start from the floor so that no one's feet get cut off as well.
> 4 If possible, let the mirror reflect the office safe. This works in the same way as it does for the cash register in a retail shop - the mirror symbolically doubles the wealth of the office.

Above: This is an L-shaped office with a sharp corner. However, the corner is not hurting the woman and the location of her desk is correct. Placing a plant to dissolve the edge of the corner is not a bad idea.

Above: Place a plant to counter the edge of a pillar that is hitting at you while you work. Change the plant when it dies or fades.

Below: A T-shaped office with two entrances facing each other is inauspicious. To help rectify the problem carefully position your desk, put plants next to the second door and use a screen to block the sharp edges of the corner.

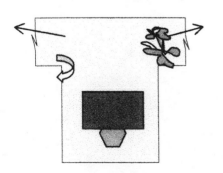

Office shapes

When selecting offices, always look for office plans that have regular shapes and try to avoid odd or irregular layout shapes. Remember, too, that regularity of shape should apply equally to all the rooms that are partitioned off in the office. Triangular, L-shaped and U-shaped floor plans are difficult to work with. Even if at the start they do not seem to be giving you problems, in the longer term they will be your undoing. You cannot be happy working in such a room and your career will not be very successful. Odd shaped rooms cause stress and misunderstandings. Anyone occupying such a room cannot hope to exert any authority in their work. If you are a manager you will have your authority completely undermined if you occupy a room that is triangular-shaped.

Squares and rectangles, however, lend themselves easily to feng shui enhancement. If you have to work in an irregular shaped space or room, do your best to regularize it. Use furniture and dividers to mark out a space for yourself and also use furniture to regularize oddly shaped angles and protruding corners. Used in this way, the office cabinet becomes a feng shui tool. Custom-built furniture is thus better than stand alone pieces. Offices with clean lines emit less bad energy than offices that have too many conflicting design lines caused by badly placed and badly coordinated furniture. Go for quality rather than quantity of space.

Try to avoid offices that have an excessive number of corners, or which have protruding corners. And try to keep overhead structural beams to a minimum; you must never sit beneath an overhead beam or sit facing a protruding corner or a pillar. You should also make sure that the pointed edge of office machines and equipment is not pointing directly at you. If there is a sharp edge facing you, move your chair a few paces to get out of the line of the edge, or place a plant on your table to act as a buffer between the pillar or corner and you. The plant will not survive for more than three months, so as soon as it shows signs of fading, replace it with another healthy plant. Bamboo rods are especially effective for countering pointed corners in the east or southeast of any room or floor space. The rods need not be very big but they should be hollow. Hanging five-rod wind chimes are helpful for corners that are located in the west and the northwest.

One of the best cures for badly shaped rooms is by using good lighting. Shining a bright light into odd-shaped corners dispels bad energy. In fact, good lighting is one of the best ways of ensuring good feng shui mainly because lights represent auspicious yang energy. But do not use spotlights. These create excessively strong energy that exhausts everyone. Hanging hollow bamboo rods tied with red string (see page 63) also helps by channelling good chi flows upwards.

Office placement

Lucky offices are never located directly facing a bank of lifts, an escalator, or a staircase. If your office is located with this arrangement, the entrance office door should be made of glass, and it should open into a fairly spacious foyer area before turning into another entrance that then becomes the real door into the office. By using a glass door for the entrance, it is deemed not to be a door. A second, more solid, door is thus necessary, and this second door can be orientated to face an auspicious direction for whoever is the manager in the office.

In fact, the best location in any office is the space that lies diagonally opposite the entrance into the office, and this space should always be reserved for the most senior person. If the office floor is large enough, as when it occupies an entire floor, this part of the office can sometimes accommodate as many as three rooms or three desk areas.

Also, lucky offices are never located at the end of a long corridor. Any such office, especially if it is a long and narrow corridor, will suffer from unfortunate feng shui. The corridor in this case acts like a poison arrow and the way to overcome this problem is to place potted plants along it, keep the corridor well lit, and hang wall paintings to break up the monotony of the corridor and to slow down the rush of chi. Placing plants along the corridor are especially good as they force the chi to meander. It also helps to hang a wind chime just above the door on the outside. I usually recommend that office corridors be made to curve.

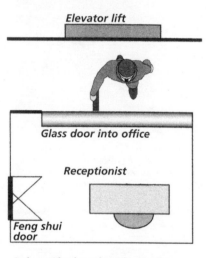

Below: An unlucky office: it is placed facing the lift.

Elevator lift

Glass door into office

Receptionist

Feng shui door

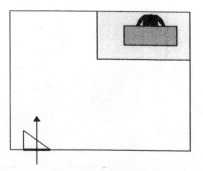

Below: The best location in the office is the place that lies diagonally deep inside and opposite the main door, as shown here.

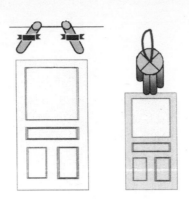

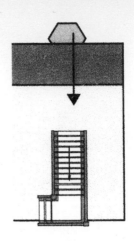

An office at the end of a long corridor is like being hit by a poison arrow.

If your office door faces another, prevent confrontation by hanging bamboo stems tied with red ribbon or a wind chime just above the outside of the door.

Do not sit facing a staircase as your luck will run down the stairs.

If the entrance to your office directly faces another office door, the chances of there being ill-feeling and lack of goodwill within the office are very high. These confrontational modes all too easily cause misunderstandings and quarrels. Try hanging a wind chime or some hollow bamboo stems just outside the door to counteract the potential problems.

The room that is placed at the end of a corridor is considered inauspicious. If the board room is located here, the entire company's fortunes suffer. If the manager's room is placed there, his or her department suffers. The bad effect is, of course, much heightened when the person sitting inside the room also directly faces the door. I would say that such a person cannot stay long at the job. He/she could either fall desperately ill or be asked to leave the company. If his/her personal luck is good, that person will resign or get a better offer from elsewhere.

If you are allocated a room that is placed at the end of a long corridor, and you have no choice but to accept it, try to position your desk so that you are not directly facing the entrance door. Then hang two bamboo stems tied with red thread just outside your door. Or if you wish (although, of course, it will be most unfriendly to do so), you can hang a small protective Pa Kua, again just outside your door. I prefer the bamboo stems.

If a room is positioned so that it directly faces the entrance of the main office, it will be inauspicious. Being too near the entrance, the occupant will get distracted too easily and consequently her or his concentration will suffer.

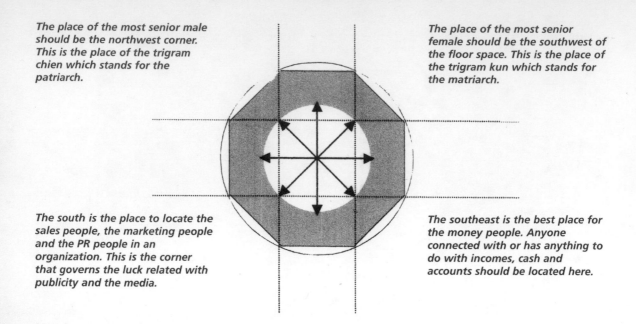

The place of the most senior male should be the northwest corner. This is the place of the trigram chien which stands for the patriarch.

The place of the most senior female should be the southwest of the floor space. This is the place of the trigram kun which stands for the matriarch.

The south is the place to locate the sales people, the marketing people and the PR people in an organization. This is the corner that governs the luck related with publicity and the media.

The southeast is the best place for the money people. Anyone connected with or has anything to do with incomes, cash and accounts should be located here.

Office layout according to the Pa Kua

Office layout can be designed to benefit the company if done according to the Pa Kua. According to compass feng shui, each of the eight directions is more suited to certain occupations and for specific types of luck. It is an excellent idea to arrange office layout to maximize feng shui luck.

◆ Northwest and southwest are extremely important locations and one way of interpreting the Pa Kua is to place the most senior man on the floor in the northwest and the most senior woman in the southwest.

◆ Place the finance department, which handles money and cash within the office, in the southeast corner of the floor space. This should enhance the company's finances and cash flows.

◆ Similarly, keep the office safe in the southeast and accountants and accounts staff are best placed here, too.

◆ The most ideal place for the marketing, public relations and sales people is the south portion of the floor space. This is the corner most conducive to generating the sort of energy needed for success in selling. The southwest is also excellent for this department.

Creating an auspicious office

Actively creating good feng shui luck is the fun part of feng shui practice. At a practical level, it involves an amalgamation of element theory with yin yang cosmology. It also requires a thorough understanding of feng shui symbolism and an appreciation of the meanings associated with the four celestial animals – the dragon and tiger, the turtle and phoenix. There are many objects which can be incorporated into the practice – symbols that represent wealth and prosperity, objects that signify long life and good health and motifs and icons that bring added luck according to dates of birth and astrological charts.

There are different kinds of luck that can be activated and various methods to choose from and to try. These will be directly dealt with in the next and final section of the book. Meanwhile, activating good feng shui in the office can be approached two ways.

Sitting orientations and directions

From the individual's perspective, sitting directions and orientations are within anyone's personal control. While you often have little or no say over the manipulation of your workspace, the sitting direction is something that any person can direct, simply by rotating your body so that you are sitting facing at least one of your four good directions.

Using the Kua number formula given on pages 72-6, I strongly urge every ambitious career person interested in upward mobility to always try to tap their best, most auspicious direction when working. Of prime importance is that you always sit facing at least one of your four good directions. As a consequence, by doing this you will naturally avoid facing one of your four inauspicious directions.

If for some reason, you cannot sit facing your best direction, try to sit facing at least one of your other good directions. This is vital since facing any of your inauspicious directions will cause you considerable bad luck. If you are unlucky enough to sit facing your total loss direction, serious misfortune could well befall you.

- It is always excellent to sit diagonally opposite the door and facing it. If you need to have your desk slanted to face your most auspicious direction, by all means do so. But never try to face your best direction if in doing so you have your back to the door. It is better to seek a compromise solution by facing a second or third best direction.
- Try to sit in a location that enables you to have the boss behind you. Even if he/she is in another part of the office, this denotes that the boss is behind you, supporting you. Never sit in a location, which results in you being placed in a confrontational position to your boss. Even though he/she may be in another part of the office, this could well create problems for you with the boss. In fact, sitting in a confrontational mode, directly facing another person, can sometimes lead to serious misunderstanding.

The use of formula feng shui must always be practised together with physical feng shui. In this connection, there are several important guidelines that should not be compromised:

- Never sit directly facing any door, but especially the door that opens into the office or into your room. When you sit directly in front of the door, energy that is too strong will hit you. You will get hurt. Always move your desk a little out of the path of energy that enters. Remember that energy that flows in a straight line can be very harmful, while energy that flows in a meandering fashion is more benevolent.
- Never sit directly facing a long corridor that is either inside or outside the office. If the corridor is outside the office, keep the office door closed at all times. To help you do this, fix an automatic door closer. If the corridor is inside the office, and you have no authority to do anything else, at least place a small rock crystal on your desk. This will have the effect of blocking the rush of negative energy that is coming directly at you.
- Do not sit facing the edge of any wall, pillar, or cabinet. The edge of any object or structure emits negative energy causing illness and misfortune. You will feel listless and be lacking in energy and you will have no enthusiasm for anything. Place a plant or keep a permanent vase of fresh flowers on your desk between you and the edge. Change the plant or flowers regularly.

Reminding yourself

A very good friend of mine who owns and manages probably the largest shopping complex in Singapore, the Ngee Ann City centre, actually draws out an arrow on his desk to make certain that he always sits facing his best direction. This is also what I did throughout my corporate years to make certain that I never forgot my directions. You can do the same.

- Do not sit directly under an exposed overhead beam, and even if it is not exposed, do not sit directly under a structural beam. Move your desk as far away as possible from the beam and then hang a pair of bamboo stems tied with red thread from the beam, or hang a wind chime. These cures help to dissolve the negative energy thereby protecting you from its harmful effects.

- Always have some open space in front of you. This allows healthy energy to flow your way. If the space in front of your desk is cramped, it is unlikely that you are getting good feng shui. If there is a solid wall in front of you move your desk back to create space in front.

- Do not sit with your back to the door. Whatever you do at the office you should never have your back to the door. This is the surest way of getting betrayed or stabbed in the back by people you trust. If you are an employer, this sort of sitting arrangement will cause you to be cheated by your employees. There will be dishonesty in your office. If you are an executive, you will lose out in a promotion, and if you are a junior office worker do beware, you could get blamed and be made the scapegoat for anything that goes wrong. Always try to move the desk so that you can see who is entering the room.

- Always sit with a solid wall positioned behind you. This assures you of important and high-powered support within your working environment – this is especially important if you are a big corporate boss. If this is not possible, and there is a window behind you, you should at least hang solid blinds or curtains behind you to simulate the support that is so vital in company life.

- Do not sit with your back to a window or you will lack support for your work. All your plans and projects simply will not meet with success and support from employees will be sorely lacking. Projects won't get off the ground, and even when they do, there will be enormous obstacles and difficulties. If you are already sitting with your back to the window, move your desk around, even if the direction you were facing was an auspicious direction.

- The only exception to sitting with your back to a window is if there is a very favourable view outside like a rounded solid mountain or a bank building! I have a friend who is the managing partner of a consultancy firm. He sat with his back to the window but behind him in downtown Kuala Lumpur was the Citibank head office of Malaysia. Needless to say, my friend has been very successful for many years and has grown enormously wealthy and successful.

Nothing beats having symbolic support. Those of you wishing to simulate such a scenario can place the picture of a bank building on the wall behind you; this would be especially good if your business requires the support of banks. Personally, I prefer Mount Everest and for many years I had just such a print behind me. Do not use a map of the world, though. It does not work. Nor should you use mountains that are too pointed or volcanoes. These are fire element mountains and they do not suit everyone. A variation of the mountain picture method is a picture of a hardy, leatherback, deep sea turtle. These creatures are known for their tenacity and the turtle symbolizes many auspicious things – longevity, resilience and strength. As the turtle isone of the four celestial creature its presence in your office is most auspicious.

◆ Do not sit with an exposed bookcase behind you. The open shelves will be like knives cutting into your back. The symbolism is very inauspicious, and apart from causing you to suffer from backaches, this arrangement could also cause you to be betrayed.

◆ Do not sit facing a staircase. Whether the staircase is going up or going down, this is one of the unhealthy arrangements. Anyone whose place of work is located between two staircases (going up and going down) will descend in a downward spiral and it will be very difficult to get up again. I know someone who had his office in a tiny room just off the landing of a staircase of a building with four levels. His luck just kept going down and became worse and worse until he moved out of that silly office.

◆ Do not sit facing a toilet door. This is a terrible arrangement since all the negative energy from the toilet will surround you with total bad luck. Stay far away from it!

◆ Do not sit facing a mirror. Better to have your back to it than to sit facing it. When you face the mirror, you will be easily distracted. Also, the mirror could well reflect sharp edges and other harmful structures that

Window views

Be aware of your window view. When you work in a high-rise building, having a window view is always very welcome as it introduces the natural environment to the work place. However, with more and more cities now becoming concrete jungles, window views can often cause problems.

To start with, don't sit at a desk that directly faces the edge of another building staring at you from across the road. This is probably one of the most serious and common feng shui problems facing office workers. You should shut out the view if this is your particular affliction. Use shades and wooden blinds rather than curtains to block the building from sight.

Similarly, if your view is of a tall, threatening-looking tower, a cross-shape façade, or a heavy television aerial or satellite dish, they are all harmful. Do not sit with your back to these types of harmful structures. Doing so merely exchanges one problem for another. If you face something that sends out bad energy towards you, the chances are that you will get ill, and your work suffer. If you put your back to it, however, you could well get stabbed in the back and be the unsuspecting victim of company politics.

Making a presentation

When making a presentation never do so with the window behind you. Always stand with a solid wall behind. Also try not to make presentations with the door behind you. This has the same effect as sitting with the door behind.

It is also recommended that when you are speaking, do not have anyone sitting or standing behind you. It is distracting and very bad feng shui for the speaker. In any office therefore, the meeting rooms and board rooms should always be designed to make sure these guidelines are followed.

hit at you without you realizing it. Move your desk so the mirror is either beside or behind you.

◆ Do not sit with water behind you. If your office has an aquarium fitted by a boss who believes in feng shui, make certain you are not sitting with the aquarium behind you. Remember that water behind is never a good thing, and in an office environment, water behind could well drown you. Instead, sit facing the water to tap auspicious good fortune.

Activating your personal space

With your office and desk laid out auspiciously you can then set about energizing your desk and the immediate space around you. Make sure your immediate space is well lit, and that it is always clean and well organized. A cluttered desk that is not properly lit cannot produce good energy. If you find that you have to squint because it is too dark, how can the feng shui be good? Conversely, if you find that you have to work under the glare of powerful direct lighting or succumb to being hit each workday by the glare of the afternoon sun, how can the energy around you be good?

Above: A desk piled high is not good feng shui!!!

Below: Bring in good feng shui from your windows. Use curtains and plants to encourage good energy.

◆ If you have a window view and it is harmful close it off with a blind. If you have a window ledge, decorate it according to what direction the window faces. If it faces east or southeast, place a flowering indoor plant. A small electrical water feature like a miniature fountain here will also create wonderful success and money luck. If the window faces south, hang a bright red curtain in front of the window. This will make you noticed in a favourable way. If the window faces west or northeast, however, hang a wind chime in front of it, and if the window faces southwest, invest in a natural quartz crystal to enhance your social life.

◆ Make certain you never have leftover food or

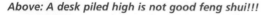

drinks on your desk. Good feng shui is something you have to work at. Keep your space clean and tidy at all times. Clear your work at the end of each day and do not pile up your desk habitually. Stacks of paper block the chi and prevent good fortune from flowing towards you.

◆ Do not sit with either your back or your front directly hit by a door, a corner, and overhead beam, a staircase, the edge of any furniture or wall. These have already been dealt with, but are repeated here to remind you that you can never have good feng shui if something very basic is wrong with your space in the first place. Take steps to protect yourself first. Practice defensive feng shui before energizing your space.

◆ Do not be seated directly under an air conditioner vent. The draughts will definitely hurt you: apart from giving you a backache, you could also succumb to illness and tiredness. Your productivity will suffer.

◆ Place a painting of a mountain on the wall behind you, to give you support. But make sure there is no waterfall or river or lake in the painting since water behind you is not a good idea. If you don't like the idea of a mountain scenery you can always energize the wonderfully lucky celestial creature – the turtle. This creature can also bring you enormous good luck so get a picture of one!

◆ Place a vase of fresh flowers on the left-hand side of your table. This simulates an active dragon. Of course, if you have a small decorative model of a dragon, you can also place it on your left.

A vase of fresh flowers stimulates an active dragon.

◆ Place a crystal or a small table lamp on the table in front of you. It would be even better if you are facing south since this energizes the fire element of the direction. Even if you are not, placing a small lamp on your office table always attracts good luck.

Lighting in the office

Lighting in the office can be designed to simulate maximum feng shui beneficial energies. To start with, all offices should be well lit. There should be no dingy corners where beneficial energy is forced to stagnate, thereby growing stale and vapid. This is what causes bad feng shui, which is manifested in illness of the staff, as well as listlessness and tiredness. Wherever possible, allow natural light to come into the office. So don't close off windows with shades or curtains. Where artificial light supplements natural light, ensure it is gentle and indirect. Lights are extremely wonderful energizers since they create precious yang energy, but they must not become too yang.

Lights can be used to brighten up dark corners, narrow corridors and cramped foyers. Keep these small spaces in the office well lighted. If your personal space suffers from inadequate lighting, invest in a small table lamp and place it on the top left-hand corner of your desk.

Good feng shui for the whole office

If you are a manager and have an interest in making the whole office enjoy good fortune feng shui, your approach needs to be all-encompassing. Thus while you need to be concerned about your own personal space, you must also be aware of the feng shui of the entire office.

To start with, an auspicious office is one that is not afflicted by the killing breath of poison arrows. It should also exhibit the fundamental basics of good feng shui. This includes having a good regular shape, an auspiciously oriented main door, a spacious entrance foyer inside and outside, and a generally good layout that does not suffer from cramped corners and long narrow corridors. With these basics in place, it is possible to introduce special features that bring good fortune to the office which benefits not just the company, but also everyone who works there.

Using feng shui dimensions in the office

esk dimensions are a vital part of good feng shui. Here are the recommended dimensions of a good feng shui desk. Please note that the desk is a large desk. Ambitious executives and managers should note that if your desk is not large enough (according to the dimensions given here), you will not enjoy good career feng shui. Tiny desks are meant for those who are not ambitious. At work, you should have a sizeable desk. Even computer workstations should not be too small. If they are, they will not bring you luck.

Above: Auspicious dimensions for a desk.
Height: 84 cm (33 in)
Width: 109 cm (43 in)
Length: 195 cm (75 in)

If the desk is too high for you, place a platform for your chair to make yourself more comfortable. The front of the desk must be closed, as shown here. Any carved or embossed decorative features should not be sharp or pointed. Instead, they should be curved or rounded. Desks made of almost any type of wood are auspicious. Do not place metal edges at the corners as this creates element disharmony.

Left: A good chair for feng shui has a high back and arm rests.

Your chair should have a high back and arm rests, as shown in the illustration. Low backed chairs lack support, and chairs without arm rests are symbolically bereft of the green dragon white tiger representation. They are definitely not recommended if you are embarked on a career path. Auspicious feng shui desks can also be designed for less senior executives. This is because of the way feng shui dimensions work.

Below: Auspicious dimensions for a smaller desk.
Height: 81 to 84 cm (32 to 33 in)
Width: 84 to 86 cm (33 to 34 in)
Length: 147 to 152 cm (58 to 60 in)

In effect, there are eight cycles of dimensions, four of which are auspicious and four are inauspicious. Each cycle measures approximately 17 in (43 cm), and each cycle is categorized into eight segments. The cycle of lucky and unlucky dimensions then repeats itself over and over again to infinity.

Those wishing to have the auspicious dimensions for smaller desks and chairs, here are the dimensions:

Amateur practitioners have often asked me for the exact length and breadth that is needed to conform to feng shui

The height of chairs can follow those of the desk, but do remember that chairs should always have arm rests to provide symbolic support.

dimensions. My answer is that there is not just one single auspicious measurement. Instead, the feng shui ruler offers a range of auspicious measurements, and those who wish to be very precise about the kind of luck they want to activate should study the feng shui ruler and the meanings given for all the auspicious and inauspicious dimensions. Another frequently asked question is whether it is the outer or inner part of the desk that needs to have lucky measurements. My answer has always been to try and apply the dimensions on inner and outer sides of desks and cabinets.

The feng shui ruler of dimensions

The four cycles of auspicious measurements given here are the precise computations that can be applied to almost anything that requires a measurement. The way to use the feng shui ruler is simply to work out the multiples of the range of measurements given as auspicious. The meanings of each of the four cycles have also been summarized to let you understand the nature of the auspicious luck indicated.

Chai: between 0 and $2^1/_8$ in (0 and 5.4 cm). This is the first segment of the cycle and it is further subdivided into four categories of good luck. The first approximate $1/_2$ in (1 cm) brings money luck; the second brings a safe filled with jewels; the third brings together six types of good luck, while the fourth brings abundance.

Yi: is between $6^3/_8$ and $8^1/_2$ in (16.2 and 21.5 cm). This is the fourth segment of the cycle. It brings mentor luck, ie it attracts helpful people into your life. As before, there are four subsections within this segment. The first approximate ½ in (1 cm) means excellent children luck; the second predicts unexpected added income; the third predicts a very successful son and the fourth offers excellent good fortune.

Above: The first sub-sector of good luck.

Above: You can use feng shui dimensions on almost anything – from cabinets to files to calling cards.

Kwan: between $8^1/_2$ and $10^5/_8$ in (21.5 and 27 cm). This third set of auspicious dimensions bring power luck and the first sub-sector means easy to pass exams. The second sub-sector predicts special or speculative luck, the third improved income, and the fourth attracts high honours for the family.

Pun: between $14^6/_8$ and 17 in (37.5 and 43.2 cm). This category of dimensions brings lots of money flowing in if it is in the first sub-sector. The next sub-sector spells good examinations luck; the third predicts plenty of jewellery, and the fourth offers abundant prosperity.

PART

4

Essential enhancements

Activating luck

Money, health, influence, or power... Happiness in relationships, romance, marriage ... Good descendants, healthy children, family. Feng shui takes care of every type of luck, and classifies them into eight main categories that find expression in each of the eight sides of the Pa Kua. But categories of luck overlap, and their context has to be interpreted in the light of modern day scenarios. The previous sections of this book have already dealt with the general guidelines of attracting good fortune for the home and for the office.

Although there are only eight sides of the Pa Kua, in this section I address nine types of luck, because I have differentiated between income luck and business luck. Needless to say, my delineation of luck into different categories is an artificial demarcation. In reality, when you activate one kind of luck, you could well be activating another related kind of luck. In my own home, because I am so greedy for all the good things of life, I actually activate every corner of my house in order to enjoy every kind of good fortune.

If that is your inclination, you can indeed do the same. There is no necessity to feel guilty just because you want every kind of luck. That, after all, is what having a well-balanced life is about. Wealth without a good family life is empty and meaningless; and love without money can evaporate and fly out the window. So my advice is for you to study every section of the rest of this book, and then systematically, go ahead and activate every kind of luck for yourself and your family.

Homes that enjoy auspicious feng shui luck are said to enjoy a balance of the eight types of luck. These eight types of luck define the parameters of a full and happy life according to the tenets of feng shui. When luck is unbalanced, however, there is something missing. Thus wealth luck without the luck of a happy and harmonious household is deemed inadequate. In the same way, a house cannot be deemed to be lucky unless there is also good health and good descendants luck. If there are no sons to continue the family name, all the success and wealth is deemed incomplete. The aim of feng shui therefore is to ensure there is an adequate balance of good fortune, and to ensure that all members of the family, and all residents, enjoy good fortune.

General safeguards already covered in this book should first be taken care of before proceeding to using the enhancement techniques suggested in this section. I cannot overstress the fact that irrespective of how excellent this part of your feng shui practice is, the enhancements are completely destroyed by the presence of just one single poison arrow. So always be aware of beams, corners, staircases and toilets. Make sure none of these things is hurting your main door, your important corners or your desk.

Feng shui for better income luck

Probably the easiest and fastest benefit for practising feng shui is to enjoy a better income. There are so many different recommendations and methods for getting wealthy that an entire book can be written on this subject alone. It is because of this that many of the feng shui experts who offer consultancy services in Hong Kong, Taiwan, Singapore and Malaysia have corporate clients. I know of a great many wealthy tycoons from my part of the world whose wealth escalated after the feng shui man had modified their homes and offices.

Water is the major symbol of money. To attract income luck, one of the best methods is to introduce a water feature into your living environment. The water feature should not be too large as to overwhelm the home – it would then be said to overflow thereby creating a situation of danger. Keep a sense of balance. In feng shui, when in doubt, less is better than more, and small is better than large.

Here are six income enhancing feng shui features you can incorporate into your home. Do remember, however, that these arrangements and objects will not be effective if your home is suffering from the attack of poison arrows, and if your feng shui defences have not been properly put into place before setting about activating good fortune.

Building a pond near the front of your house

Let the pond have a radius or diameter of between 41 and 43^1/$_2$ in (104 and 110.5 cm) or between 49 and 52 in (124.5 and 132 cm). These dimensions signify a jade belt and a roomful of money. It is not necessary to make the pond any larger than the largest of these dimensions. Also make certain that the pond is placed on the left-hand side of the main door. The direction is taken standing on the inside of the door and looking out.

If the pond is placed on the right-hand side of the main door, income luck will still flow into the home, but in addition to income luck, it also brings the luck of additional wives and concubines. Remember in the days of old China, the practice of feng shui was always done to benefit the family patriarch. Remember also that in those days, a successful man usually had several wives and concubines, and indeed, the more wives he had, the more successful he was deemed to be.

Of course, today things are quite different, and it is important to recognize this fact. Tap the water to improve your family's income, but let the benefit be for everyone. Otherwise, while incomes improve, wives also run the risk of losing their husbands to another woman. This very important principle holds true whether or not the pond is built inside or outside the home. It must be on the left of the main door!

To enhance the feng shui of the pond, design the flow of water so that it keeps running all the time. This creates precious yang energy. Moving water is said to represent great good fortune so invest in a small pump to recycle the water, and a filter to ensure that the water stays clean. Dirty water brings poisonous breath.

Japanese carp should be kept in multiples of nine.

Keeping some fish in the pond will generate additional yang energy. In feng shui, the fish itself is a symbol of abundance. During the Chinese New Year, eating raw fish is said to signify great abundance throughout the year, and ceramic and brass renditions of the carp are popular decorative items for the house. Japanese carp (known as koi) kept in multiples of nine would be excellent feng shui enhancers for the pond, but avoid buying koi that have a red dot on their forehead as these are said to symbolize failure.

If you cannot afford carp, you can keep other kinds of fish, except for the angular angelfish. Angular fish are said to represent a loss of income. If your fish die on you, there is no need to panic. Simply go to the pet shop and replenish. There is a superstitious belief that says that when otherwise healthy fish die on you, they have absorbed bad luck which otherwise would have befallen you.

If keeping fish proves to be too much trouble, you can also decorate the pond with water lilies, and successfully planting the fabulous lotus is said to bring enormous great good fortune. The lotus is both an auspicious and a sacred flower, and Buddhists the world over regard the lotus as one of the eight secret treasures.

Keeping a tortoise in your north corner

The tortoise can be a real live tortoise or a fake ceramic model and it can be a tortoise, turtle or terrapin. The presence of any member of the tortoise family symbolizes the presence of this celestial creature in the home, and his presence brings both wealth and great good fortune. The tortoise brings money as well as the assistance of helpful people. His traditional place is the north, which is also the place of the water element, so it is a good idea to place the tortoise in a container of water.

Tortoises live both in and out of water and it is a good idea to create a small landscaped tortoise pond if you have a garden. Feed them with fish food or pellets, or with watercress or other green vegetables. If you live in an apartment, identify the north corner of your living room, and place your tortoise arrangement there. It is not necessary to keep more than one of this celestial creature. In fact, you should never keep them in a pair because they are said to prefer being alone. One is the number of the north.

Keeping an aquarium of goldfish in the southeast corner

To energize wealth luck it is an extremely good idea to keep goldfish in the living room, especially in the southeast. The aquarium should not be too big, rather it should simply be large enough to keep nine goldfish comfortably. Of the nine, one should be black to symbolically absorb any bad luck meant for you. Keep the aquarium bubbling with water because it is the bubbling water that attracts the prosperity chi into your home. If you are engaged in business, place a light shining into the aquarium so that flickering shadows are reflected onto the ceiling. This signifies active turnover for your business, thereby increasing your sales and consequently your income. Aquariums are especially suitable if you do not have a garden, and for apartment dwellers.

Goldfish are especially good for energizing wealth luck if positioned in the southeast.

Round, tubular aquariums are better than square ones, but any shape that is regular would be acceptable. In the Far East, superstitious business-men like keeping what they term the feng shui fish, the arrowana, which is a freshwater tropical fish. Unfortunately, they cost so much, you need to be rich already to afford one.

Placing a jade plant in the southeast

This is a succulent form of cactus plant. It has no thorns and has fleshy leaves in a deep shade of green that resembles the precious jade. In fact, any kind of round or heart-shaped leafy plant can represent the money plant. Place it in the southeast because this is the corner that signifies prosperity. A live plant energizes this area because the southeast is of the wood element.

If the southeast also happens to be your personally auspicious direction based on your Kua number (see pages 72–6)

Left: The leaf of a jade plant; a plant positioned in the southeast attracts prosperity.

then you must definitely energize this corner of your living room since the benefit is greatly strengthened for you. Even if the southeast is not one of your good directions, and is instead one of your inauspicious directions, you should still energize this corner since everyone in the home benefits from it. It is perfectly acceptable for you to place auspicious feng shui objects or symbols in any corner or sector of your home whether or not the sector is personally auspicious.

Creating a small waterfall in your garden

If you have a garden in front of your house and this is not the south part of your land, you can build a small waterfall feature in front of your main door to attract great prosperity luck.

Design the feature so that water flows towards your entrance. It is important for the water to flow towards your door rather than away from it. When water flows away from your door, it carries luck away from your home. When water flows towards your front door it brings luck towards you. The waterfall should be about 10 to 15 ft (2 to 4 m) away from your door, and it should be on the left-hand side of the door (inside the house looking out). It should not be too large – its size should be proportionate to the door.

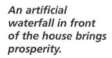

An artificial waterfall in front of the house brings prosperity.

Having this waterfall feature can bring exceptional wealth luck, although this luck does not come in the form of a windfall. Instead, the waterfall brings you one or two outstanding opportunities to become seriously wealthy. Thus it also brings a lot of hard work and sleepless nights as you go about transforming the opportunity into something tangible. In short, waterfalls create the catalyst for small-time entrepreneurs to hit the big time and become serious business tycoons in the making. Feng shui brings genuine opportunities. How you make use of these opportunities depends on your own luck and the depth of your own ambitions, aspirations and determination.

Hanging a bright light in your foyer

If you hang a chandelier in your foyer to welcome chi into your home, it brings wonderful auspicious luck. In feng shui, water and fire are at two opposite ends of the element spectrum (water destroys fire), but they are also the two elements that must be energized to attract the luck of wealth and riches. The best arrangement is to have a view of water outside, and have an auspicious brightly-lit entrance area. Chandeliers are excellent, especially when made of crystal (see page 87), as these create a harmonious blending of earth and fire energies, but any kind of bright lamp is suitable.

Feng shui for better romance luck

One of the most superb applications of feng shui is the way it seems to be able to work wonders making marriages happy again. It makes relationships between spouses come alive, brings new friends into dull, lonely lives, and energizes opportunities for marriage for those who keep missing out on finding meaningful relationships and partners willing to commit to each other.

I have seen feng shui help a great many couples to find themselves and have seen it save many marriages on the verge of collapse. As a result, I am now a firm believer in feng shui's potency in the area of romance and personal happiness.

The secret of using feng shui to ensure a happy family and love life is to understand the great importance which feng shui places on household happiness. In all of feng shui's many guidelines, there is always a special section which addresses this aspect of human aspiration. And in accordance with the Chinese view, the key to family happiness lies in the strength of the matriarchal spirit. Marriage, love and family all revolve on the quality of the matriarchal energy within a home.

This is condensed within the trigram kun that is symbolized by three broken or yielding lines, and represented by the direction southwest. Thus, one way of safeguarding the family happiness and togetherness of the home is to protect the southwest corner of the home.

Protecting the southwest

The major thing to remember about safeguarding the matriarchal energies of the southwest is that there should never be a toilet placed in the southwest corners of the home. When the attached bathroom of the master bedroom is placed in the southwest corner of the room, the marriage or relationship of the couple occupying the room is sure to come unstuck, it is bound to split apart.

If the guest toilet of the home is located in the southwest corner, then the sons and daughters (but especially daughters because we are dealing with female energy here) of the household will have a hard time getting married. Even if they do get married, if they continue to stay in the house, their marriage will be unhappy and be full of stresses and strains.

The only way to deal with a toilet being in the southwest and systematically flushing away the family's love and marriage happiness is to not use the toilet altogether. A possible way of correcting the situation is to place a mirror on the door of the room containing the toilet and to keep the door shut at all times by fixing an automatic door closer.

Energizing the southwest outdoors

There are several methods of strengthening the matriarchal energies of the southwest corner outside the home. Since the intrinsic nature of the southwest is of the earth element, and since feng shui is tapping earth luck, the key to energizing the southwest is to embellish the earth energy of this corner. Here are two ways, which, however, require you to have a garden.

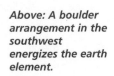

- ◆ Place decorative boulders in the southwest corner. Then, against a wall or corner in the southwest, make an arrangement of nine boulders, with two boulders more prominent than the rest. Tie a red string around the two larger boulders. Or decorate these two boulders with the double happiness character written in red paint. If you like, you can light up this corner during the night time hours. This method activates the earth energy of the garden, creating auspicious energies to those in need of a little love and romance in their lives.

Above: A boulder arrangement in the southwest energizes the earth element.

Below: A hollow pole with a light at the top end energizes the southwest bringing marriage opportunities and romance into your life.

- ◆ Sink a hollow pole into the ground, and have a light installed at the top of the pole. Let the pole be hollow and sink it into the ground for at least 3 ft (1 m). Above ground the pole should be at least 5 ft (1.5 m) tall. The light at the top of the pole draws the earth energies from deep within the ground, and then channels it upwards. When done correctly, this envelops the garden and the home with wonderful earth energy which again brings restful romantic luck to members of the household. Daughters of marriageable age will have no problem meeting men with honourable intentions and sons will find wives with no problem.

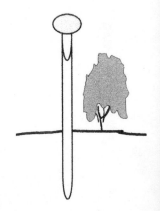

Energizing the southwest indoors

If you live in an apartment, there are two excellent methods for energizing the luck of the southwest to benefit your overall love luck.

- ◆ Hang a happy family portrait on a living room wall that is either itself positioned in the southwest corner, or try to engineer the composition of the family portrait and have everyone in the picture face towards the southwest. Actually, just hanging a family portrait in the home creates happy vibrations if every member of the family is smiling and happy. A happy portrait in the southwest strongly emphasizes the family as a loving unit, thereby strengthening the luck of the matriarch.

◆ Place crystals and lights in the southwest of the living room. Either natural quartz crystals or artificial lead crystals will create the necessary energy for activating the southwest. I personally prefer the natural variety, but crystals used for feng shui purpose should be well lit for at least three hours each day. I recommend that you shop around for lamps that have some kind of crystal feature. Or look for lamps that have energy saving features to enable you to have them turned on the whole day.

Romance in the bedroom

Sleeping in your nien yen direction could well require you to orientate your bed in an awkward way. My advice is to go ahead and do it if you are having serious family or marriage troubles. It will definitely alleviate your unhappiness and even help you to solve your problems. But you must make sure that in so doing, you do not inadvertently end up sleeping under a beam, facing a door or being hurt by the poison arrow of a protruding corner. These would affect your luck even more seriously.

Remember, too, that sleeping between two doors makes you quarrel a great deal with your spouse and sleeping between two pillars makes you irritable and stressed. Both will destroy your marriage luck.

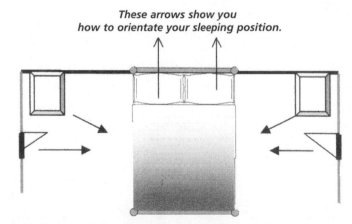

These arrows show you how to orientate your sleeping position.

Sleeping between two doors makes you quarrel a great deal with your spouse and sleeping between two pillars makes you irritable and stressed. Both will destroy your marriage luck.

Improving some marriageable prospects

In 1996, I visited an old friend in the United States whom I had not seen for well over 20 years. It was a reunion of sorts and I met his three stunningly beautiful daughters, Meg, Mary and Ann. They were in their late twenties, had great careers and seemed, on the face of it at least, perfectly happy. But I soon discovered in the course of our conversations that all three daughters were still single with not a prospective husband in sight. I also discovered that while the girls were not unduly worried, their Mum and Dad were. Bill's wife, Angela, asked me if there was anything wrong with their home. Why, she wanted to know, were her girls still single? Meg, the oldest, was already 31, and Ann, the youngest, was 26.

The answer to Angela's question was easily diagnosed when I asked to borrow their rest room. I discovered this guest toilet of theirs was located smack in the southwest corner of their rambling ranch-style home. It was not the only toilet in the southwest either. Directly above the toilet on the ground floor was another.

A toilet in the southwest of the house flushes away all the romance luck of the home. It is not merely the marriage chances of the sons and daughters of the home that get hurt. It also creates marital problems between husband and wife. This is because the southwest of any home is the corner that governs the luck of family relationships. The southwest is the place of the matriarch, of mother earth. The trigram of this direction is kun, which is the ultimate yin trigram. If this corner is sullied by the presence of the toilet, it hurts female members of the family more than the males.

I told Angela to stop using both their toilets in the southwest. It was not an easy thing to ask of them, but feng shui is getting increasing acceptance in the United States and Angela was determined to become a grandmother. Because they had a large house, they complied with my request. And just to make certain (because I wanted to show them that feng shui would really work), I also activated their romance luck in the garden. This was done by turning on the light in the southwest corner outside for the full 24 hours of each day. To be even more certain, we moved a couple of large boulders into that corner, and tied a red ribbon around the boulder to energize the luck of mother earth.

I am happy to report that Meg has just become engaged to a doctor and I shall be attending their wedding in February next year. Mary has started dating someone seriously, and her mother is very hopeful.

Feng shui for better children luck

Good family luck includes the happiness of having children and seeing them grow up safe, healthy and sound. If you are childless and seem to be having a hard time conceiving, even though the doctors say there is nothing wrong with either you or your husband, you can suspect that perhaps something is not quite right with your feng shui. Actually, this was what happened to me and my husband.

For the first nine years of our married life, we had been afflicted by bad feng shui caused by a very large casuarina tree that grew 3 m (10 ft) from our front door. As if that was not bad enough, our main door was also not solid as it had two glass panels. We had such terrible feng shui. At that time I was already well acquainted with feng shui, and had started learning about it. But like all beginners of this great science I missed the wood for the trees. I was so caught up with the theory behind feng shui, and so keen to find out if it worked that I completely missed seeing the tree in front of my door. Later on, it was Mr Yap, my expert feng shui friend and teacher, who told me that as long as we lived in that old house of ours we would never have a child. The poison arrow of that tree, he said, was too strong to overcome so we should consider moving on.

When we started plans to build our own house, we decided to use feng shui to help us have a baby. Mr Yap taught me how to position our master bedroom to tap my husband's descendant luck corner. This was his nien yen, or romance, direction. According to Mr Yap, the romance direction is also excellent for enhancing descendants luck. In addition to orientating the bedroom, we also positioned the bed so that both of us slept with our heads pointed to my husband's nien yen direction.

In case there are women readers wondering why we had to use my husband's direction, and not mine, the answer is that to activate descendant's luck to use feng shui to help you get a child, you must follow Chinese convention and use the man's favourable directions. Not the woman's.

Anyway, four months after moving into the new home I conceived my daughter, and Jennifer was born in our tenth year of marriage. After trying unsuccessfully for nine years to have a baby, we finally succeeded.

Those of you who are childless for no known medical reason, and desperately want a baby, might want to try using feng shui to see if it might help. Refer to the Kua numbers on pages 75-6 and from there, determine the 'nien yen' direction of your husband. This will be his third good direction. Next identify the room in your home that is located in this direction. Use that as your master bedroom, and both of you should sleep with your heads pointing in his nien yen direction.

Selecting rooms for your children

For your children to benefit from good feng shui, it is not necessary to use their personally good feng shui directions until they become teenagers. When they are still young, they will benefit from the overall good feng shui of the home, or suffer if the feng shui is generally bad. It is thus not necessary to use Kua formula feng shui for them until they are much older. Naturally, if you are able to accommodate the different auspicious directions of every member of your family (including those of the children) then everyone enjoys good feng shui. If this is not possible, then what I am saying is that you may compromise on the directions of the children.

Children will enjoy excellent feng shui if they are given rooms in the east part of the home. More specifically, sons, and especially the first born son, should be given a room that is located in the east sector of the home while daughters, and especially the eldest daughter, should be given a room in the southeast sector of the home. The east and southeast have wood as their intrinsic element and the main characteristic of the wood element is that it represents growth. Wood is the only one of the five elements that has life and is able to grow.

East is also the place of the green dragon. Planting lush greenery on the east side of the home benefits the young children of the family tremendously. Or place a small ceramic green dragon anywhere along an east wall of the home. This will also bring wonderful yang energy and an abundance of sheng chi, or growth energy, into the home, benefiting not just the children but the whole family as well. In the Forbidden City in Beijing in China, all the young dynastic princes lived in palaces located in the east, while the older members, including all the old concubines of the Imperial family, were placed on the west side. In addition, to reflect the green dragon's abode, and to denote the wood element, roof tiles of the palaces located in the east were coloured with green glaze.

If you have a large family and there are several sons and daughters, you should keep the eldest boy and eldest girl in the east and southeast respectively, but for the other children, follow the Pa Kua's guidelines. This places the girls in the south and the west. The middle daughter will benefit from a room in the south while the youngest daughter will shine if given a room in the west. The middle son should be given a room in the north while the youngest son will benefit from a room in the northeast.

As the children get older and reach puberty, it is a good idea to investigate their respective Kua numbers and to then allocate rooms for them according to their individual auspicious directions. This ensures they grow up sturdy and strong, and that they stay a part of the family. Homes that enjoy good feng shui seldom have problems with rebellious or difficult children.

Yang feng shui for children's rooms

In the arrangement of furniture and selection of colours for your children's bedrooms, be very aware of yang energy. To ensure that your children grow up with an enthusiasm for life, and are motivated towards attaining the ambitions that bring honour and good name to the family, it is important that they benefit directly from plenty of yang energy. It is not necessary to be subtle, so observe the following guidelines:

◆ Let their rooms be well lit and with no dark corners.
◆ Use bright, solid colours or white for their walls.
◆ Do not let their rooms get overly damp, use a dehumidifier if necessary.
◆ Introduce sound into their rooms by giving them a radio or a hi-fi player.
◆ Create movement with clocks and other toys.
◆ Let there be a presence of books to symbolize the acquisition of knowledge.
◆ Make certain there is at least one window, and air it daily.

Auspicious objects for a child's room. Place a bright lamp and hi-fi system in the room to raise yang energy. A globe in the southwest and horseshoe magnet under the bed bring extra luck.

Also, make sure that you do the following:

◆ Ensure rooms are cleaned and tidied up each day.
◆ Keep hostile toys like guns, tanks and so forth tucked away in cupboards.
◆ Undertake spring cleaning at least once a year.

Feng shui for improved health luck

An important component of good fortune, irrespective of social or material status in life, has to be the luck to live a long and healthy life; a life that is free of debilitating and soul destroying diseases that weaken the physical body. Feng shui addresses the health aspect of good fortune directly in two ways.

First, almost every feng shui compass formula offers a specific direction geared towards attaining just this type of luck. In the orientations and directions formula given on pages 75-6, this is the doctor from heaven or health direction. Thus feng shui offers a distinct direction for orientating your sleeping and eating habits as a method for improving failing health. Usually, you will find that when other major aspects of home feng shui are correct, energizing this health direction for sick people can lead to an improvement of their condition.

Secondly, in the realms of symbolic feng shui practice, there are many symbols signifying long life, which when displayed in the home are said to bring about this aspiration for residents of the household. The Chinese are extremely conscious of longevity, and there are those who regard it as the most important aspect of good fortune. Great reverence is always accorded to Tai Chi and Chi *kung* masters. These health *si fus* teach postures and exercises that ensure good circulation of chi, and good balance of yin and yang within the body. Their exercises follow the same principles on which the practice of feng shui is based, and indeed can be considered to be a branch of feng shui, the branch that focuses on the flow of chi within the human body.

In the old days, emperors concerned themselves with the continuing search for immortality, and Chinese legends are full of stories that describe this search. One of the most popular of Taoist legends, for example, describes the Eight Immortals, and many Chinese families display paintings of this legend in their home. There are probably more emblems of longevity than of any other of life's aspirations. Many of these are lavishly carved onto furniture, drawn onto wall paintings and decorative screens,

The deer is a popular symbol of longevity.

and stamped onto ceramic and porcelain ware. These symbols are freely displayed in Chinese homes because longevity is considered a major manifestation of great good fortune.

The ritual of moving house

To get off to a good start in any new home, select a good day and date for moving in. The Chinese usually consult the *Chinese Almanac*, or *Tong Shu*, an annually updated calendar which describes good and bad days for doing just about anything, but which, unfortunately, is written in Chinese. This book is an annual best seller in Hong Kong and other countries of the Far East.

Consulting the Almanac to choose auspicious dates is a way of life with the Chinese. Selecting good dates for moving house is part of feng shui.

On moving into a new home, do the following: switch on the lights, turn on a tap, boil some water, make some tea, and have a small meal.

The selection of auspicious dates based on the feng shui tools of analysis – the Lo Shu square and the Pa Kua – is a specialized branch of the practice that requires special study. It is usually not necessary for beginners to learn this branch of feng shui. Those who need to select good dates can ask friends who have access to the Almanac. If this is not possible, then select dates that are at least not harmful. Two days that are definitely not harmful, and which are generally regarded as good dates are the first and fifteenth days of each lunar month. This coincides with the days of the new moon and the full moon.

On the designated day for moving in to your new home, try to undertake the official entry into the new home between the hours of nine and eleven in the morning. This should be regarded as the official move into your home. Bring in the bed or at least one big piece of furniture that signifies you are moving in; then turn on the radio to create some noise level, boil a kettle of water and open wide a window (see box, below). Make yourselves a cup of tea and serve some biscuits. This will be your first meal in the new home and you must make sure that you stay the night after moving in. Having done this symbolic moving in, you can take your time to move in the rest of your furniture and possessions.

Clear the air of stale energies

On the day you move in, clear the energies by opening all the windows and letting the air flow through the house or apartment for at least three hours. This will effectively clear the home of stale and tired energies left behind by previous occupants. Turn on all the lights and turn on the taps to signify a flowing out of old energies and a flowing in of new ones. You should also have given the house a good scrub before moving in. Having any home redecorated, or at least repainted is also excellent. Changing the carpets and wallpaper are activities that introduce new energies into the home, energies that are fresh, healthy and very yang.

Observing this ritual takes care of the time dimension of feng shui, and when the ritual of moving in is observed as directed, it is supposed to ensure that your family's stay in the new home will be peaceful and healthy. If shortly after moving in to a new home your family starts becoming sick, you can be sure that the moving in day must have been inauspicious.

Energizing for good health and longevity

There are specific feng shui techniques for energizing the luck of good health and longevity, and for avoiding the bad luck of sickness within the home. Listed here are four important guidelines to follow:

Countering excessive yin energies

If you live near a hospital, a cemetery or other places that emit strong yin energies, you could suffer bad luck in the form of sickness. Each person in your household could take turns getting sick. When yin energies become excessive, or when the source of such energies are too near, residents could even have to be hospitalized.

To counter excessive yin energy, introduce the symbols and representations of yang energy into your house. Install brighter lights; paint your main door a bright red colour, and turn on the music. Introduce some bright colours – red, orange and yellow, even white – into the overall decor of the home. The secret of a healthy home whose residents enjoy good health is when yang energies are dominant yet well balanced with yin.

If your house directly faces a building such as this, your feng shui is already badly affected; but if this building is also a hospital, the bad feng shui is seriously compounded.

Deflecting the shar chi of poison arrows

Another common cause of ill health caused by bad feng shui is when the house, and especially its main door, is being attacked by the killing breath or shar chi of poison arrows coming from across the road, or from a neighbour's house, or from a neighbouring building. Defensive feng shui requires developing sensitivity to the harmful structures of the environment. Again when your home falls prey to such structures, the first thing that happens is that the health of the family suffers.

Block or deflect the harmful energy being sent towards your home by planting trees or building a barrier like a wall or a hedge. Blocking off the sight of the offensive structure is considered good enough to dissolve the bad energy coming from it. If it is difficult to do either of the cures suggested, you can hang a Pa Kua mirror over the main door.

Displaying longevity symbols

If you want to enjoy a long life, use feng shui to bring you the luck of longevity, which implies good health. Do this by displaying longevity symbols both in and outside the home. Inside the home, the best symbols to display are paintings that depict the peach, the pine tree, the bamboo, the crane or the deer. These are the classical and most popular symbols of longevity. They are often shown together in paintings and other decorative objects sold in Chinese emporiums. To the Chinese, of course, the most powerful symbol of longevity is the God of Longevity, or Sau.

Outside the home, go for the tortoise or crane. Garden statues of these creatures symbolize harmony and longevity. Place them anywhere in the front part of the garden for the cranes and at the back part of the garden for the tortoise. There are some exquisitely well done statues of long life cranes that are available at garden shops. A single crane is sufficient. Planting a bamboo grove on the right-hand side of the front garden is also an excellent symbol of longevity and good health. Any species of bamboo is acceptable. Meanwhile, if you live in a colder climates, I recommend you plant a pine tree by the side of your home. This is not only a symbol of good health and long life, it also represents fidelity, strength and unwavering loyalty in the face of adversity. The pine tree is one of the most awesome of feng shui features to have around any home. However, as with all things, it is never wise to be excessive. One pine tree is quite sufficient. Keep things balanced at all times.

Above: The crane is one of the most beautiful symbols of longevity.

Below: Bamboo always represents good feng shui. If you have the space, grow a bamboo grove near your home to bring you

Sleeping with your head pointed to health direction

The health direction is generally regarded as the second best of four auspicious directions (see page 75). Under normal circumstances, most people prefer to sleep with their head pointed towards their best direction since this brings the promise of material success in business and career. But if you are ill, and you need to recover to enjoy your wealth, then my advice is that you should sleep with the head pointed to the health direction.

Sleeping to tap the health direction also brings peace of mind and great harmony within the family. It is not always necessary to utilize the best direction all the time. The direction you choose to energize should be determined by your life situation at any moment in time.

Feng shui for better education luck

Education has always been regarded as one of the best ways of moving up the social and success ladder. In China of the old days, scholars were especially highly respected. Most parents aspired to have sons who could bring honour to the family by attaining scholastic achievements of the highest levels. This was because the emperor's advisors and court officials – the powerful mandarins, who ruled the land – were always selected from among those who passed the Imperial exams with high honours.

Feng shui was therefore always assumed to include this kind of luck for the sons of the family, whose luck is seldom seen in terms of only a single generation. Good fortune has always been defined in terms of the family enjoying generation after generation of wealth, social prominence and prosperity. For this reason, sons and heirs were required for the continuation of the family name. Descendants luck was thus crucial, and wives who could not bear sons were usually cast aside to make way for secondary wives or concubines who could.

Once the lineage of the family is assured, the next kind of luck that becomes important is the luck of education. In a Chinese family, sons especially are always expected to be good at their work in school. They are expected to proceed to college and university to become scholars, and to pass their examinations with flying colours. This attitude and expectation is firmly ingrained into the psyche of Chinese families, and perhaps this explains why immigrant second generation Chinese Americans do especially well in universities. Apart from having been brought up with a tradition that reveres education, many also probably benefit from good education feng shui arranged by their parents.

Living with three summits

An interesting belief associated with educational attainment for the next generation which I picked up on one of my visits to China describes great good fortune for families who live with a view of three summits in the distance. These three summits represent great educational honours and successes for the sons of the family. It is believed that the old family home of Deng Xiao Ping had just such a view in the distance.

Crossing the dragon gate

A colourful reminder of the old days is the symbol of the humble carp crossing the dragon gate (lungmen). After swimming against the current all the way to the gate, the humble carp makes one mighty leap, jumping to successfully cross the gate and be transformed into a dragon. This legend of the dragon carp symbolizes the successful passing of Imperial exams. Chinese families familiar with this legend display the dragon carp above their main entrance doors to symbolize successful educational attainments for their sons and, in modern times, their daughters as well.

The humble carp becomes a dragon after successfully crossing the dragon gate. Those who did not make it, forever bore the stamp of failure – a red dot on their foreheads.

Energizing the northeast

Those keen on energizing education luck for their offsprings can try any one of several feng shui methods. These can be practised singly or in combination to enhance education luck for your children. Pa Kua feng shui pinpoints the northeast as the sector that signifies educational attainment. Thus, energizing this corner will enhance education luck for your children. The best way to do this is to introduce all or any of the following features into your children's bedroom – for both sons and daughters.

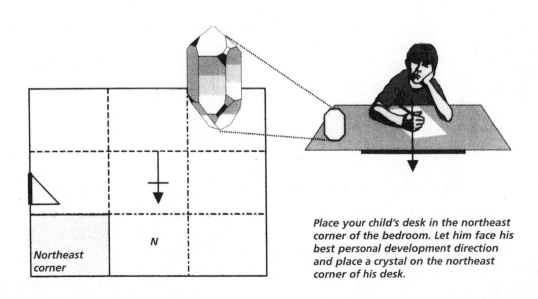

Northeast corner

N

Place your child's desk in the northeast corner of the bedroom. Let him face his best personal development direction and place a crystal on the northeast corner of his desk.

Placing your child's desk in the northeast corner of the bedroom

Place the desk where your child does his/her homework in the northeast corner of the bedroom. Please note whether any bathrooms or toilets attached to the bedroom are placed in the northeast corner of the room since this would tend to have quite severe consequences for your child's scholastic and school career. If the bathroom is placed in the northeast of the bedroom, it might, if possible, be a good idea to find another bedroom for your child.

Letting your child face his or her best personal development direction

With the desk placed in the education corner, the next thing to do is to orientate the desk such that he/she sits facing his/her personal growth direction. In Chinese, this is known as the *fu wei* direction, and it is an excellent direction to energize for anyone who is a student. If you cannot do anything else, just doing this one thing would make all the difference.

In fact, this is one of the most excellent methods for helping your son or daughter become a straight A student. Refer to the tables on pages 72–6, and check out the different auspicious directions for your son or daughter based on the date of birth and gender. Once you know what the best direction is for your child, teach him/her how to energize it for studying, for working on assignments, for sitting in the classroom and, if possible, for taking exams.

As far as possible, try to tap the personal development direction. If that is not possible, then make sure your child is at least facing one of the other auspicious directions. At all costs avoid facing one of the four bad directions. So, even if you cannot tap the direction you ideally want, you must always make sure you are not facing any of your four bad directions.

Placing a crystal on the northeast corner of the desk

The third thing to do is to activate the energies of the element of the northeast. The ruling element of this sector is earth, and I have discovered the best object to use for the purpose of improving education luck is the natural quartz crystal. Place it on the tabletop in the northeast corner of the desk and, if possible, just underneath a table lamp. This strengthens and charges the crystal.

Crystals are believed to have tremendous retentive capacity and memory power and can be acquired from any New Age crystal shop. They can be used to create good feng shui. Placing them in the earth corner is an enhancing technique of tapping good feng shui energy. I have passed this method on to so many of my young friends with great success. Needless to say, my own daughter has also benefited from this method.

Get one crystal for each child and encourage your children to look after their crystal carefully. When they are revising or doing their homework, place the crystal on the table. When they are in class or listening to lectures, bring the crystal along and place it on the northeast corner of their desk in the classroom. And when they are taking their exams, encourage them to take the crystal and place it on the northeast corner of their exam desk.

I do not guarantee that everyone who uses this method of energizing their desks will become a straight A-student overnight. But I do say that there will be a steady improvement of grades. If all other types of luck are also auspicious, then high educational attainments become a real possibility.

Be careful of what is underneath the staircase

A major feng shui taboo that must be observed by everyone with children is to watch what is placed under the staircase. Anything unsuitable or harmful placed here creates bad luck for the next generation. The most dangerous feature placed here is a water feature. Any kind of water feature placed under the staircase breeds enormous bad luck for your children. Doing badly in school is just one of the bad things that could occur.

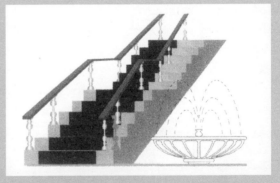

Any kind of water feature placed under the staircase breeds enormous bad luck for your children. Doing badly in school is just one of the bad things that could occur.

So never place water under the staircase. A pond, fountain or aquarium, no matter how arty or fashionable, would be quite lethal in their effect, and the danger is most directly focused on the descendants of the household. Things become worse when the staircase is located in the centre of the home because then the ill luck extends to the whole family. Water under the staircase destroys the foundation of the home, and wipes out descendants' luck.

It is also not a good idea to keep the space beneath the staircase empty. Turning it into a storeroom and keeping things there symbolically creates a strong foundation for the whole house. When I decided to become a writer, I turned the bottom of my staircase (which was located in the centre of the house) into a small storeroom for my books. Needless to say, this generated tremendous luck for me in my new occupation.

Feng shui for better opportunities luck

The essence of feng shui benefits lies in the abundance of opportunities that will come your way when you arrange your living space in accordance with its principles. This is the essence of feng shui luck. Almost every technique and method you use to improve the feng shui of your home or office will bring you wonderful opportunities to enhance your wealth, your happiness and your lifestyle.

But it is also possible to use feng shui to open new dimensions that enhance the aspirations and ambitions of every resident in your household. This brings different things to each member of your family. For those engaged in a business, the technique brings wonderful new opportunities for expansion and improved efficiency. For those pursuing a career, it brings fresh openings for upward mobility and for catching the eye of influential and powerful people. For job seekers, it brings additional openings for gainful employment, and for students, it substantially broadens the horizons.

Those who seem to have had a spell of bad luck, with everything going wrong, my advice is to try energizing this aspect of feng shui luck. It involves activating the south corner of the home, so the first thing to do is to identify that part of your house or garden.

Energizing the crimson phoenix

The south is the place of the crimson phoenix (see page 26) and it is a remarkable symbol of good fortune. In feng shui, the phoenix is in the south. The view from the main door should be of this creature, crouched on the ground ready to take off. This can be represented by a small mound that can resemble a little place for you to rest your feet. Often, a small boulder is sufficient to create the necessary symbolism. If all of this is sounding very figurative, that is exactly what it is. Thus if you have a small mound of earth placed a little

Even a small boulder can represent the phoenix if placed in the south and in front of the home.

away from your main entrance, and if this represents the south part of your land, then you would have successfully energized the crimson phoenix. It will attract opportunities with great potential for you and your family.

Substituting the phoenix

If you do not have a garden, you can also activate the energy of the phoenix inside your apartment. Consider your living room as the space you wish to activate. Determine the south corner of the room, and in that corner place a ceramic or crystal image of a phoenix, and then light it up with a red glow of light. If you cannot find a phoenix, you can select from any number of substitutes. Personally, I use the rooster because this too is an excellent symbol. The rooster may not possess the magnificent lineage of the phoenix but it is also regarded as a hugely beneficial object to have in the home. This is especially the case if you were born in the year of the rooster (see pages 72-4).

You may also display a peacock to great effect. The peacock in full display of its stunning plumage is regarded as a symbol of great good fortune. In many parts of India and Nepal, the peacock is regarded as a bird that brings opportunities for the patriarch of the household to rise to positions of great prominence and influence. Its intrinsic qualities thus mirror those of the phoenix. It is believed also that simply displaying peacock feathers in the home will attract good fortune. I have some in my home, and I place them in the south corner of my family room on the upper level to attract good luck for my daughter.

A rooster makes a good substitute for the phoenix.

Placing a bright light in the south

There is another way of attracting the luck of opportunities. This requires you once again to identify the south corner of your home, and to install a very bright light in that corner. I love using crystal chandeliers for this purpose and have used this method with notable and continuing success. In the south corner of my living room, of my foyer, and also in front of my main door, I have hung small crystal chandeliers that energize the fire element of the sector and also entice the good fortune sheng chi into my home. I have found that every member of my family is never short of fresh opportunities to enhance our lives – whether it is materially or spiritually.

It is not necessary to choose elaborate expensive chandeliers. Instead, go for the single bulb models that have at least nine golf-ball sized faceted crystal globes. The faceted crystal balls are very efficient for catching the light from the bulb, and then breaking the light into rainbow colours that transform all surrounding energy into auspicious and happy sheng chi. Keep the chandelier turned on during the evenings for at least three hours. You will see a huge difference in the feel of your living room as well as the rest of your home.

Crystal chandeliers are so good as a feng shui tool because the energies created synthesize in a harmonious fashion – fire and earth, a productive relationship that also signifies many of the major components of the luck syndrome. If having a chandelier is too much for your budget, then I suggest you buy one crystal and hang it near the window so it can catch the natural light from outside, and bring the light into the home. See if your home has windows that are orientated in a way that allows you to have the crystal catch the morning sunlight from the east, sending rainbows towards the front door or foyer. This brings a great deal of opportunity luck.

Placing a red or gold wall hanging in the foyer

It is considered extremely auspicious to place a wall hanging that has red and gold as the dominant colours on the wall that directly faces the main door. This can be calligraphy of the single word 'luck' or 'patience' in Chinese, or a painting with an auspicious theme. The red and gold colour combination signifies abundance and great good fortune, and having it just inside the home near the front door attracts excellent chi flows into the home, bringing with it exciting new opportunities for the residents.

Feng shui for enhanced assistance luck

The Chinese take a very pragmatic approach to the pursuit of success and material gains. In business and in politics, they divide the people in their life into those who can help them and those who can hurt them. Good fortune is often expressed in terms of the presence of people who can and will help them; while bad fortune is when there are people in your life who can hurt you.

The luck of having the guidance of an older, wiser and more experienced person – someone who may be a teacher, a supervisor, or a boss – is a widely recognized form of feng shui luck. This is often compared to the good fortune of having a benevolent patriarch looking after your career progress within a large organization. This patriarch (or matriarch) figure may be your own father/mother, an uncle/aunt, or just someone with whom you have developed a kind of mentor-protégé relationship. Indeed, it is regarded as extreme good fortune when you get a supporter like this in your life, and in feng shui terms this sort of person is described as a 'heaven man'.

The most potent method of attracting this quality of luck into your life is by understanding and energizing the premier trigram of the *I Ching* and the Pa Kua. This is the trigram chien, designated by the symbol of three solid lines. This trigram implies help, luck, and blessings from heaven. It also represents the leader, the patriarch, the boss – anyone who is directly important and influential to your family or your household. For a country, the trigram chien represents the President or Prime Minister. For a corporate entity, it signifies the big boss. In a religious order, it represents the Pope or spiritual director. Chien always symbolizes help from the most important person in your life and focusing on chien in the home and office places you at an advantage over your peers.

Amplifying the energies of the chien corners in the home

Doing this means enhancing the northwest corner of your house or office, and you can do this using several different objects.

Using bells

If you are in business or engaged in a profession that requires the goodwill of many people, hanging a pair of metal bells in the northwest corner of the room would be most auspicious. If there is a door in that corner, place the bells on the door so that it announces someone's arrival. This is an especially good feature to add onto the entrance doors of small shops and boutique operations. Apart from announcing customers, the chimes of the bell also ensure that the beautiful sounds distract bad luck away from the premises.

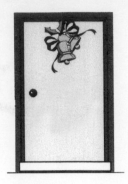

Placing a metal horse shoe

Burying a horseshoe made of steel in the northwest part of the garden is said to energize excellent earth energy as it produces the metal element energy that signifies the northwest. Keep the horseshoe in a small container before burying it in the ground. The symbolism of this particular practice is that the horseshoe will bring helpful assistance speeding to your home.

Tie red ribbons on bells hung on a northwest door to energize the effect of the bells' metal element.

Enhancing a missing northwest corner

Those engaged in business and politics would feel the lack of a northwest corner most acutely. My advice to friends suffering from this missing feature has always been to find another place where the feng shui is more conducive to the success of their ambitions. This is because a missing northwest corner would mean a complete absence of assistance in any form from influential and powerful people. No businessperson or politician can

The bad luck of empty spaces

No home can have good feng shui when the house stands on empty space. Even when only parts of the home suffer from this feng shui affliction, you should investigate which rooms these are.

Rooms placed above empty spaces cannot enjoy good feng shui. If the vital and important northwest rooms of the home are above empty spaces like a garage, or if the house is built on stilts as shown to the right, the luck cannot be good. You must fill up the empty space. Close it up with walls and turn the space into utility rooms.

A house built on stilts with empty spaces exposed like this suggests a house with insufficient foundation. Fill up the space by building walls and creating rooms in this part of the house.

Overcoming a missing
northwest corner

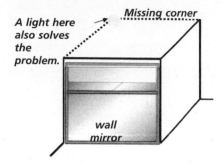

A light here also solves the problem.

Missing corner

wall mirror

succeed without this kind of patronage luck. There are, however, several ways of correcting a missing northwest corner.

♦ Use a full length mirror placed on one of the walls of the missing corner. This visually extends the wall outwards suggesting substance and space. The only exception to the use of this cure is that it cannot be used in a bedroom, and it cannot be used if the mirror reflects a toilet, a staircase or a door.

♦ Install a light in the missing corner. This is a solution that can be used only if you have a garden, and you have enough space.

♦ Instead of a light, extend the corner to regularize the shape of both the room and the house.

♦ Perhaps more drastically, consider extending into the missing area.

Feng shui for better business luck

In Hong Kong, businessmen who follow feng shui faithfully consult the expert at the start of each lunar New Year to investigate the good and bad months during the following twelve months. If the calculation indicates that the timing is good they will launch new projects, expand and announce major new strategies. When the timing is bad, they lie low, keeping a low profile until the bad stars fly out of the natal charts of their buildings or homes.

Businessmen know there is a time dimension that complements the spatial dimensions of feng shui. These time calculations are based on complicated formulas that offer numerological clues to the state of luck of buildings and on directions and locations. If you are in business, you might want to look for a practitioner who is well versed in flying star feng shui to work out the time luck of your building, your office, your shop and your home for the next twelve months.

The charts on pages 72-6 are sufficient to alert you that things could go wrong for you if either your office, work desk or main door is located in a specific sector that has bad luck stars. This is all that is necessary in a general introductory book such as this. For more detailed calculations of the flying stars of your office, you will either have to get my detailed book on flying stars feng shui (entitled *Chinese Numerology in Feng Shui*) or employ the services of an expert who is able to draw up the natal chart of your office building or shop.

Attracting better business luck

An easier approach to using feng shui to attract business luck is to implement form school recommendations. These have been devised by master practitioners and have proved workable over many years for their many thousands of clients. Methods of feng shui enhancement are usually based on symbolism and on application of the five-element concept.

Good feng shui for any business begins with good feng shui for the boss. This means the owner in privately owned businesses, and the chief executive officer in publicly held companies. The location and orientation of the boss's personal space, the placement of his/her desk, and the direction of his/her sitting position are the three basics to get right.

Feng shui knowledge should be treated as an additional management tool. This was always my approach during my corporate working days. I would almost always work at getting the feng shui of all my staff as auspicious as possible, particularly during my Hong Kong banking years.

Make an effort to ensure that everyone working for you and for your company sits in his or her respective auspicious orientations (see page 75). Just remember that it is not possible for everyone to get all three of the basic guidelines correct. But if each member of your team receives help from at least one basic feng shui fundamental, your whole company benefits from the generally harmonious interaction of energies.

Other aspects to consider such as the position of your office and desk placement have been covered in greater detail in Part 3 (pages 137-49).

Energizing money luck

The presence of water in the form of miniature fountains and goldfish aquariums are a common sight in the offices of Chinese businessmen in Hong Kong and Taiwan. The entrepreneurs of Hong Kong especially, are serious practitioners of feng shui. Most are careful about observing advice given by their feng shui masters, particularly advice that has to do with the material success.

Chinese businessmen place commercial and material success at the top of their list of aspirations. Because of this, fish and decorative water products are invaluable additions in their office decor. There are several versions of recommendations when it comes to water. Some advise that water should be visible from the main entrance into the office, maintaining it is the visual sight of water that attracts money luck into the office. Thus you will see offices that have fish tanks placed in the reception area of the office, directly facing the entrance. In Hong Kong, goldfish are extremely popular, especially the lion-headed goldfish which is believed to symbolize both protection and prosperity. In Malaysia and Singapore, sea water coral fish are more popular than goldfish as these are easily obtainable from the tropical coral reefs around the coastlines of Malaysia.

Right: Water in the form of an aquarium energizes money luck.

Another popular fish, which is generally regarded as the wealth fish, is the highly priced and prized arrowana. Those of you who wish to use this

Good feng shui for Phillipines and Singapore?

Some years ago, a well-connected friend of mine from Hong Kong informed me President Ramos of the Philippines, determined to break the spate of bad luck afflicting his country under his predecessor Cory Aquino, had consulted a feng shui master from the colony. The feng shui master told Ramos to do three things for the Philippines to prosper.

First, Ramos was to get rid of three offending trees in front of Malacanang Palace. The trees were blocking the success of the president and once they were cut off, there would be nothing blocking his good fortune.

Secondly, Ramos was to change the Philippine 500 peso note. There were too many unlucky features in the note.

Thirdly, Ramos was to change the symbols on the presidential seal since this, too, had too many unlucky features, including a sea lion that had a crooked tail.

We all know that President Ramos has had an exceedingly successful presidency. Was it due to feng shui? Who knows?

A better story comes from Singapore.

On the island of Singapore, lives a very influential man. He is learned and wise, and has great respect for his Chinese traditional roots and culture. He is also said to be particular about feng shui, thus there is a particular day and time of the day to inaugurate an impor-

tant event. There is also a particular colour of his dressing, when it comes to important occasions, and so on. He has a feng shui mentor in the person of a famous monk, a particular Venerable who died recently. This man would seek the advice of this Venerable whenever he had to make an important decision.

Now, at around the time when the Mass Railway Transit construction was taking place on the island, the one dollar coin came into circulation. Apparently, the Venerable had advised the learned one that the MRT tunnelling work had caused bad feng shui for the island, and its prosperity could be diminished. Determined to push ahead with the project anyway, he asked if there was anything that could be done to circumvent the bad feng shui.

'Yes,' replied the Venerable, 'but it may be impossible to implement.' To our hero, nothing was impossible, so he says to the Venerable, 'please speak anyway.' The Venerable then advised that every household on the island was to have, or should display, the Pa Kua symbol, which is the octagonal eight-sided shape which all practitioners of feng shui are familiar with. Oh no, there will definitely be racial riots! How can every household be forced to have a Pa Kua at home?

feng shui fish to bring enormous business luck your way should look for these fish in the markets of the Far East. They are expensive, but you do not need to get more than one. A single arrowana is potent enough. There are also several varieties of arrowana, but I personally prefer the type illustrated overleaf. Notice that the tail ends in a single fin and the whole fish looks like a sword which is said to symbolically cut away all the bad luck and obstacles facing you. Please note that the arrowana is the businessman's feng shui tool. You do not need it if you are not engaged in business. There are easier ways of harnessing money luck!

'Hey hey,' says the wise man, 'I can make everybody want to have as many Pa Kuas as possible.' Thus was born the Singapore one dollar coin. Those of you readers not from Singapore should ask a Singapore friend to send you a one dollar coin and you will see that it is shaped like a Pa Kua!

The story has a sequel …

As many of you must know, the economy did not, in fact, recover, and it did not do quite as well as expected even after the circulation of the one dollar coin – remember the 1985-86 recession?? – so the Venerable was consulted again.

This time the Venerable said that while the one dollar coin did indeed symbolize the Pa Kua, it had no effect since everyone had it in his pocket. Since the Pa Kua was not displayed how could it counter the bad chi caused by all that tunnelling. Thus was born the next novel idea – the road tax label!

Singaporeans will recall this road tax used to be a disk. It used to be round and now it is octagonal, and it is displayed by everyone all around the island. Does this innocent looking disk explain the many years of booming economy Singapore has been experiencing? What about now then? With all this turmoil in the currency and stock markets swirling around the region, Singapore surely is bound to be affected. But the Venerable is no longer around. What is to happen?

The answer lies in the Singapore fifty dollar note. This note shows the President Sheares flyover across the mouth of the Singapore river. I have been told that when this flyover was built, it caused the mouth and head of the Singapore Merlion to be injured, thereby creating enormous bad luck for the place. It was then, so the story goes, that the Venerable gave his final piece of advice. It would be his legacy to the people of Singapore for what he was to recommend would safeguard the fortunes of Singapore for a long time.

The Venerable told his long time friend to introduce a dragon on the top right-hand corner of the fifty-dollar note. The dragon would balance any harm done to the mouth of the river, and forever bring prosperity to the island nation. And, indeed, if you look for it the dragon is there, on every single fifty-dollar note. This dragon is scattered through the length and breadth of the island, bringing prosperity and success.

The dragon is also a protective symbol. It protects against ioss and poverty. I am not overly surprised that Singapore seems to be weathering the market turmoil considerably well, and will continue to do well in the years ahead. Once again, fact or feng shui?

Placement of water

A popular school of thought on the placement of water follows the five element theory which recommends that water should be placed in the north (the corner that represents the element of water). Water is also said to be most auspicious when placed in the wood corners of the east and south-east because water produces wood in the productive cycle of the elements. Since the southeast is generally regarded as the money corner in feng shui, placing water here, especially if it is also the place of the front part of the office or shop, is deemed very lucky indeed.

Arrowanas and me

I had five of these wonderful fish and kept them in a huge aquarium in my living room, placing them on a special diet so they would grow fast and long, and develop the golden, pink scales that are said to bring great wealth luck. At that time, I had just bought into the Dragon Seed department store group in Hong. Kong and had taken over as chairman of the company. I needed all the success luck in the world. My arrowanas did not fail me.

Within 18 months, my partners and I in the leverage buyout deal successfully cashed out allowing me to go into retirement. I made plans to return home to Malaysia and was offered a fortune for my five arrowana. I turned down all offers to buy my precious fish, and released them all, now 45 cm (18 in) long and stunningly beautiful, into the Stanley reservoir as a mark of gratitude for all the money luck they had brought me.

The highly prized arrowana.

Keep a sense of balance. Do not think that the more water you have and the larger your aquarium, the better it will be. When water becomes unbalanced, when there is too much, then water is said to overflow its banks, and this transforms good feng shui into bad. The element of danger is inadvertently triggered. This is exactly what happened to an acquaintance of mine. He was the chief executive officer of a large company, who when told about the wonderful benefits of water feng shui, had a gigantic freshwater aquarium installed in his office. The aquarium completely dominated his floor space and it was not surprising that barely three months later, he lost out in a boardroom proxy battle and was thrown out. So, never have a water feature that dominates the space. Too much water simply drowns you and/or your company!

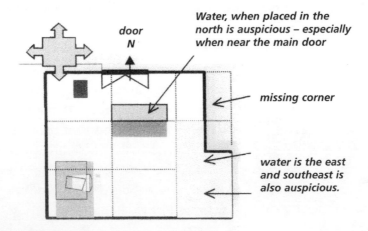

door
N

Water, when placed in the north is auspicious – especially when near the main door

missing corner

water is the east and southeast is also auspicious.

Energizing money luck with coins

I have recommended the coin method to so many people I have lost count. Every one of them who has sceptically followed one or other of the three business orientated tips I reproduce here has benefited and has become a great fan. The Chinese have for so long talked about the enormous good fortune that these ancient Chinese coins bring to households and to businesses that it has passed into the realm of superstition in many families.

Three Chinese coins tied together, yang side up.

For years, I have placed three Chinese coins at the bottom of my rice urn, and faithfully changed them on the eve of each lunar New Year because my mother told me many years ago this would bring huge good luck for my family. These coins are not difficult to find in the Far East, and they can be found in most Chinatowns in the West. You should make certain you get those that have a yang side and a yin side. The yang side has four Chinese characters, while the yin side has two.

The coins are very thin and round, and there is a square in the centre. The combination of the round and square shapes represents the auspicious union of heaven and earth. It is not necessary that these coins should be antique although those that have come from the Chien Lung period of the last Ching dynasty are quite highly prized because this was considered the most auspicious time of the Manchu period.

You will need to tie the three coins together, yang side up, with red string or red ribbons. This activates the prosperity potential of the coins. There is no special method for tying the coins. Simply make sure that all three coins are yang side up and they have been transformed into wonderfully potent feng shui tools.

Taping coins onto files and invoice books

Stick three coins on your important files to enhance turnover and sales luck.

Stick these three coins, yang side up, on all your important contract files and on your invoice books to enhance your turnover luck and increase your sales. This is one of the easiest and most effective way of energizing the business luck of these coins. Distribute them to your sales and marketing people to energize their turnover luck. You can tape the coins on all your important income generating files. Place them on the sides as shown in the illustration to the left. This ensures the coins can be seen. This same method can be applied to cash boxes and safes to symbolically enhance the amount of cash inside. In fact, I strongly recom-

mend every retail establishment to have this feature incorporated into their feng shui practice. The effect can be quite breathtaking as you see your business picking up. You can also tape these coins to the entrance door of retail shops, or just inside the shop above the door.

Some feng shui experts recommend these coins be placed under a mat just inside the main door of shops and houses to attract wealth luck. I know of a very successful and large British retail chain of department stores and supermarkets that has these coins buried under their shop floors. I place them in my rice urn, on all my important files, hanging from the latch on my front door, and under my Chinese God of Wealth.

Positioning the cash register in retail establishments

In retail shops, the most important corner of the shop is where the cash register is placed. First, note where you should not put the cash register:

◆ Never place it directly under an exposed overhead beam or directly facing a protruding corner or knife-edge of two walls. The cash register should be given the same amount of care and consideration as the main door.

◆ Directly in front of the door as it should not be the desk that a customer sees as soon he/she walks in.

◆ Facing a toilet, a staircase, or the sharp edge of a display cabinet.

To energize the feng shui of the cash register:

◆ Place a wall mirror next to it which has the effect of doubling the daily turnover of the shop.

◆ Hang a pair of hollow bamboo stems tied with red ribbons above the cash register. This creates auspicious energies using the channelling method. If there is a beam above the cash register, the two bamboo stems should be able to deflect the bad energy away from the register. Some experts use bamboo flutes and wind chimes. These are also auspicious objects and are excellent. But do not do too many things. Select what method you wish to use and stick to one method at a time. Remember that in feng shui you should never be greedy and overdo advice given.

Afterword

There are those who attribute the happiness of my personal and professional life to the manifestation of my excellent heaven luck. I was born lucky, they say. Many others are convinced my good fortune is due to the excellent feng shui of my home – my earth luck. I like to think the successes I have had in my life are due to heaven and earth luck effectively combined by my own mankind luck. Yes, I consciously and determinedly learnt feng shui and have successfully energized every corner of my home and office, as well as activated all my directions in almost everything I do. I have written this book to show you how you can do the same to create some really spectacular luck for yourself.

I discovered feng shui early. After ten years of a childless marriage, I gave birth to Jennifer after we moved house and after having had the new home feng shui-ed. The feng shui of our new home had been done by feng shui expert, Mr Yap Cheng Hai, whose track record for creating multi-millionaires make him a living legend here in Malaysia. We still live in the same house except it has been massively transformed over the years, in line with our improving circumstances.

Mr Yap was an authentic feng shui master who was also my kung fu master and my friend. Over the years, the depth and breath of feng shui expertise that he has passed to me has taken my breath away. This has been supplemented by wonderful knowledge acquired during my Hong Kong years. Mr Yap treated me like a younger sister. He was also clairvoyant and often claimed to have been my big brother in several past lifetimes. This perhaps accounts for his magnificent generosity in sharing precious formulas, fine points, and feng shui secrets with me. I truly must thank him.

A great deal of what Mr Yap has passed to me has found their way into my books on feng shui, and especially into this particular book, Feng Shui Essentials, the existence of which is due to the tenacity of Judith Kendra, who cam to my home while visiting Malaysia last year. Judith asked me to write a comprehensive text on feng shui that would be a fully illustrated and complete introduction to the subject. I jumped at the chance to be published by a major international publisher. Judith and her edit and design team, including Emma Callery and Jerry Goldie, have created an excellent, beautifully edited and cleverly designed book which presents feng shui in an easy to read and easy to apply format. I am very proud of this book.

You can apply all the tips contained in this book almost immediately. Moreover, when you have mastered the basics of the practice, you will discover that feng shui will appeal to your common sense, as well as your sense of balance, order and harmony. You will observe that there is nothing mysterious, psychic or instinctive about feng shui. It is a practice, which can be mastered easily and effortlessly – which is why there are so many 'wannabe' feng shui practitioners around these days.

I prefer to do my own feng shui and I advise you to take the same approach. Apart from outside consultants being every expensive these days, you should not be so ready to allow the privacy of your home to be violated by perfect strangers, no matter how well meaning they are.

Use this book to do your own feng shui. I promise you it will be easier than you think. It is also a lot more fun making your changes stage by stage. Let the practice of feng shui be an ongoing thing. I have been decorating and rearranging furniture, and thus changing the feng shui of my home, every year for the past twenty years. I have gained in confidence over the years when I see that everything I do to energize my corners or to activate my directions really does bring positive results.

It is this continuous success that gives me the confidence to encourage you to do your own feng shui and to have fun while doing it. I also recommend that you approach feng shui as both an art and a science. It is an art in that it requires judgement, which gets better with experience. It is also a science. There are precise specifications that can be followed and exactly applied. Get the application correct and you will feel the positive results of feng shui. If it does not seem to be working, check to make certain you have indeed got your measurements and readings correct.

It is completely unnecessary to see feng shui as either a spiritual or a religious practice. And do not be obsessive about it either. Feng shui is not and should not be the cure-all for everything. It is a powerful supplement to your luck. But it does not account for all of your luck. There is nothing New Age about feng shui – it has been around now for more than 3500 years. Feng shui is also not magic. Take this healthy attitude to feng shui and you will easily benefit from the luck of the earth.

Lillian Too

Index

Tables are shown in bold